Amanda Haas

CREATIVE COSPLAY

Selecting & Sewing
COSTUMES
Way Beyond Basic

stashBOOKS®

an imprint of C&T Publishing

PUBLISHER: Amy Barrett-Daffin

CREATIVE DIRECTOR: Gailen Runge

ACQUISITIONS EDITOR: Roxane Cerda

MANAGING EDITOR: Liz Aneloski

EDITOR: Beth Baumgartel

TECHNICAL EDITOR: Helen Frost

COVER/BOOK DESIGNER: April Mostek

PRODUCTION COORDINATOR: Zinnia Heinzmann

PRODUCTION EDITOR: Jennifer Warren

ILLUSTRATOR: Valyrie Gillum

PHOTO ASSISTANTS: Gregory Ligman and Kaeley Hammond

COVER PHOTOGRAPHY by Alex Brumley of Alexandra Lee Studios

COSPLAY PHOTOGRAPHY by Alex Brumley of Alexandra Lee Studios, unless otherwise noted

INSTRUCTIONAL AND SUBJECTS PHOTOGRAPHY by Estefany Gonzalez of C&T Publishing, Inc., unless otherwise noted

Published by Stash Books, an imprint of C&T Publishing, Inc., P.O. Box 1456, Lafayette, CA 94549

Library of Congress Cataloging-in-Publication Data

Names: Haas, Amanda Dawn, 1988- author.

Title: Creative cosplay : selecting & sewing costumes way beyond basic / Amanda Haas.

Description: Lafayette, CA : Stash Books, an imprint of C&T Publishing, 2020.

Identifiers: LCCN 2020005799 | ISBN 9781617459054 (trade paperback) | ISBN 9781617459061 (ebook)

Subjects: LCSH: Costume. | Sewing. | Cosplay.

Classification: LCC TT633 .H33 2020 | DDC 646.4/3--dc23

LC record available at https://lccn.loc.gov/2020005799

Printed in the USA

10 9 8 7 6 5 4 3 2

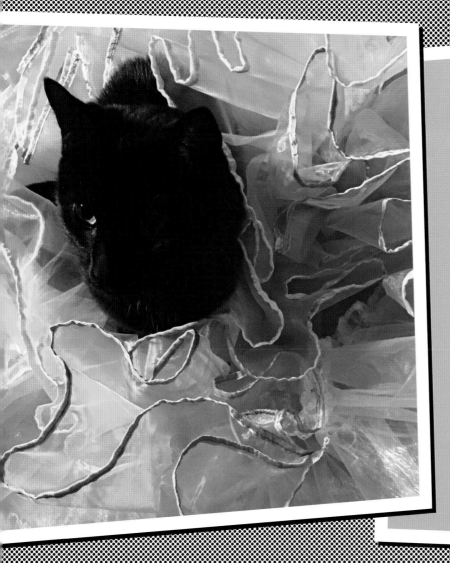

Dedication

Thanks to my beautiful cat, **SALEM**, for always being the best fabric weight and my consistent sewing companion.

To **MOM**, **DAD**, and **OLIVIA**, who all have supported my weird hobby to this day.

To my boyfriend, **JEREMY**, who has kept me going by believing that I could write a book—even if my college English class grades told me I probably shouldn't.

To all my **COSPLAY BESTIES** nationwide, who keep inspiring me every day with their cosplay creations, kindness, late-night chats, and post-con dinners.

To my **NON-COSPLAY FRIENDS** who still find what I do interesting and cool enough to share my Instagram handle.

Acknowledgments

My sincere thanks to **ALEX BRUMLEY** of Alexandra Lee Studios for providing much of the photography in this book—particularly the amazing and inspiring photos of so many cosplayers. Alex has a way of bringing a character to life while retaining the individuality of the cosplayer. Alex and I have been friends for years, and I just can't thank her enough for helping me bring my art to the masses with her photography. Thank you, photo wizard!

I also want to thank **BETH BAUMGARTEL AND THE ENTIRE TEAM AT C&T PUBLISHING**. This book would not be possible without you all. Thanks for believing in me!

CONTENTS

INTRODUCTION

Cosplay is a relatively new—and quickly becoming popular—hobby that many people are dipping their toes into. It's super fun to try, no matter your level of crafting skills. Cosplay can easily take over your brain. Before you know it, you are creating art! Cosplay is a very creative art form once you learn more about how to come up with ideas, what materials to use, and some very basic sewing skills.

As a cosplayer, with a cosplay name of Jedimanda, I get *tons* of questions almost daily about every aspect of cosplay. I love to teach future cosplayers and help anyone wanting to create their first (or their hundredth) cosplay. To better help future cosplayers, I wrote this book intended for the beginner cosplayer and beginner sewist. Cosplay and sewing go hand in hand, so you do need a bit of sewing knowledge to craft your costumes. That said, once you start creating cosplay costumes, your sewing skills will improve as you get more involved with the creative process. I hope this book inspires you and helps you start and love your cosplay journey!

COSPLAYER: Jedimanda
COSTUME: Ahsoka Tano
from *Star Wars*

COSPLAYER: Jedimanda
COSTUME: Captain Marvel
from *Captain Marvel*
WIG: Created by Custom Wig
Company using human hair

COSPLAYER: Jedimanda
COSTUME: Doctor Strange from *Doctor Strange*

WHAT IS COSPLAY?

If you ask people about cosplay, they seem to draw a blank. Some say it's a Japanese pop-culture thing; others think it's a Halloween-type event that happens at comic book conventions. Both are right in a sense. *Cosplay* is an ultimate art form in which players create costumes, accessories (including body paint and makeup), and just about anything and everything else they can think of to represent a fandom. (*Fandom* is the word used to describe the subculture of a certain pop culture subject, like a movie or video game.) Cosplayers even develop original ideas with fantasy twists—it's amazing!

Merriam-Webster defines *cosplay* as "the activity or practice of dressing up as a character from a work of fiction (such as a comic book, video game, or television show)." This is an extremely accurate definition; however, I would like to add that most cosplay portrays characters from every aspect of fantasy and sometimes nonfiction. Real-life character portrayals are becoming more popular as cosplay becomes more mainstream. Let's go back a bit and see where and why cosplay began.

The History and Psychology of Cosplay

Throughout history, humans have dressed up for all kinds of occasions, from attending a masquerade ball at the Palace of Versailles in France (during the reign of King Louis XIV), to dressing for Carnival in Rio de Janeiro for the first time in 1723. Most people did, and still do, refer to this as *costuming*. Fast forward to the early twentieth century, when authors started creating fandom worlds. People fell in love with the intellectual properties of manga in East Asia and science fiction in the West. Fans developed the first fandoms.

The term *cosplay* wasn't used until 1984. According to an article in *The Artifice*, an online magazine, Japanese reporter Nobuyuki Takahashi had attended Worldcon in Los Angeles. When translating the word *masquerade* for his Japanese readers, he thought the word sounded too old-fashioned and he coined the word *cosplay*.

THE PSYCHOLOGY OF COSPLAY

Cosplay is hard, and I will repeat this mantra throughout this book. Creating is hard, portraying characters is hard, and wandering through a convention center in cosplay is hard, but it is so worth it. With that said, there are positive and negative aspects to every hobby, and while I don't want to discourage anyone from becoming involved with cosplay, being upfront about the nature of it is important.

Anyone can cosplay—literally anyone. If you can sew a pillow, you can cosplay. If you can smile in front of a camera, you can cosplay. It's a true hobby for the people. However, practice makes perfect, and everyone starts out as a beginner. I had bit of a different beginning route because of my college schooling, but I'm still learning. It is important to understand that starting cosplay is just the first step in a lifelong adventure.

Note: My First Cosplays

My very first cosplays were Darth Maul from Star Wars *and Kitana from* Mortal Kombat 3. *When I made these costumes, I was just a beginner; it was the first time I had used body paint and spandex fabric. It was hard for me to create these costumes because I had zero knowledge or training in sewing and using body paint. I read a lot of blogs on the internet to help me through. However, I thoroughly enjoyed each costume I made, and both outfits will always have a special place in my heart.*

Escapism

Cosplay is a form of good escapism. A hobby that lets us escape from our daily life, even if just for a weekend, can be a great asset to our mental state. We can lock ourselves away in our craft rooms. We can avoid the news of the day. We can even fantasize about our upcoming conventions during our nine-to-five jobs. I wouldn't say cosplay gives us a purpose, but it has been known to help people through tough times, both mentally and physically.

Sometimes that feeling of escape can take over. One year I made fourteen different cosplays. It was an intense time and ultimately too much escapism for me. It began to feel like I wasn't creating anything worthwhile. I was working full time, and slamming out cosplays every month was derailing my social life. I was making costumes just to be part of a group for one evening at a random convention; it wasn't fun for me anymore. I needed to take a step back. Escapism was conquering my life and I had to reenter reality (which was also hard). This break made me realize that instead of cranking out outfits for social media gain or a photo-shoot opportunity, I wanted to focus on well-developed builds and original designs. Once I established this new goal, my cosplay escapism came back to me and it felt good. I found myself again as an artist. So be careful how much you escape—cosplay is flexible!

> *Note*
> *I use the term* build *often in this book. The term is used within the cosplay/crafting community to refer to a "work-in-progress project" and can encompass everything, from sewing to prop work to special-effects makeup. People talk about their builds in their social media and forum chat.*

Dealing with Social Media

I can't talk about the psychology of cosplay in today's world without touching on social media. Most people have some online presence on Facebook, Instagram, Twitter, Snapchat, and/or TikTok. There is a social media format for everyone. Cosplayers love to share their work, so our natural instinct (besides being on the convention floor) is to post our work on social media outlets.

Post and share your work! Cosplayers love to follow builds and see final photos. It gives us inspiration and motivation. Just try not to compare your work with other cosplayers; everyone starts creating at different points in their lives. Don't dwell on comparison. That can have a negative impact on both new and experienced cosplay creators.

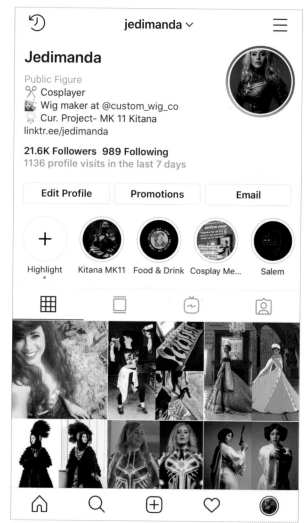

Social media is a great way to chat with fellow cosplay buddies. We want to see each other succeed in builds and designs, and if we can, we like to help with research and act as sounding boards for bouncing ideas. I've made so many friends through cosplay by first meeting them online and then happily meeting them at a convention. My cosplay buddies are some of my best friends, and I make new friendships every day in the cosplay community. A great way to start chatting with other cosplayers is to find a fandom-based cosplay group on Facebook. There are so many out there.

LEFT TO RIGHT: April Gloria, Malicious K Cosplay, Alexandra Lee Studios, me, Casey Renee Cosplay

ONLINE COSPLAY GROUPS

Some of my favorite online Facebook cosplay groups include:

- SheProp! Community (a forum for women and LGBTQIA+ creators of all skill levels)

- Kamui Cosplay Community (great group for foam, armor, and fans of Kamui Cosplay)

- Cosplay Marketing (a marketing information group to help better your marketing game)

- CosLadies Community (a female-centered cosplay forum best for sharing your work)

LEFT TO RIGHT: AngiViper, me, LunarLyn

It is important to mention that by posting our work we open ourselves to both negative and positive feedback from random internet strangers. It's up to us to comb out the negativity and fill our feeds with positivity. It's an unfortunate occasion when someone gives you a negative, hurtful, and shaming comment on the internet. I have yet to meet a cosplayer who hasn't endured some sort of hurtful social media comment. It's no fun, but it does happen. If it happens to you, block and ban the sender. All social medias have that option—use it!

Grace "Zonbi" Herbert as Lone Wanderer from *Fallout 4*

"I would argue a modern 'cosplay career' is nearly impossible without social media. Social media has definitely changed my life for the better—but there is such thing as too much *social media. Social media can be damaging if we're on it too much. Constantly taking in feedback (both good and bad) can be overwhelming. It's easy to internalize negative comments and compare ourselves to others. Taking breaks from social media and using it less has made me a happier and more grateful person!"* —Grace Herbert (Zonbi Costuming), veteran cosplayer

Costuming and Cosplay Careers

While most people that cosplay are hobbyists, there is a smaller percentage of us that do this as a career and can monetize this strange but wonderful hobby. Some of us are a cosplay personality as well as a crafter; others have opened commission shops because of their background in cosplay creation. Some have even moved to the film industry to work in prop creation, special effects make-up, or costume work. It's heartwarming to see people succeed in a career they cherish because they simply started making costumes in their own home. It's a possible route if you wish to pursue it. You have to hustle though!

Sunday Riley product endorsement photo shoot

Cover of *Cohaku* magazine

Cover of *Cosplay Culture*, December 2018 / January 2019 issue

Casey Renee Cosplay's award-winning cosplay from TwitchCon 2018: Best in Show

Cowbutt Crunchies's award-winning cosplay from The Crown Championships of Cosplay at C2E2 2019, First in the World

Cosplay as an Art Form

Because people sink their time, money, and life into cosplay, it has transformed into a true art form. There are a lot of amazing craftspeople around the world that have made insanely beautiful works of art. Even if the art project is fandom based or an original design, the result can be museum worthy. Some of my creations have been featured in an art gallery, many friends have created internationally known cosplays, and many have won worldwide competitions with their creations.

There is no end to what you can do with cosplay. Don't limit yourself, and always be open to learn. Now let's go learn about how to make your first costume!

CHOOSING YOUR COSPLAY COSTUME

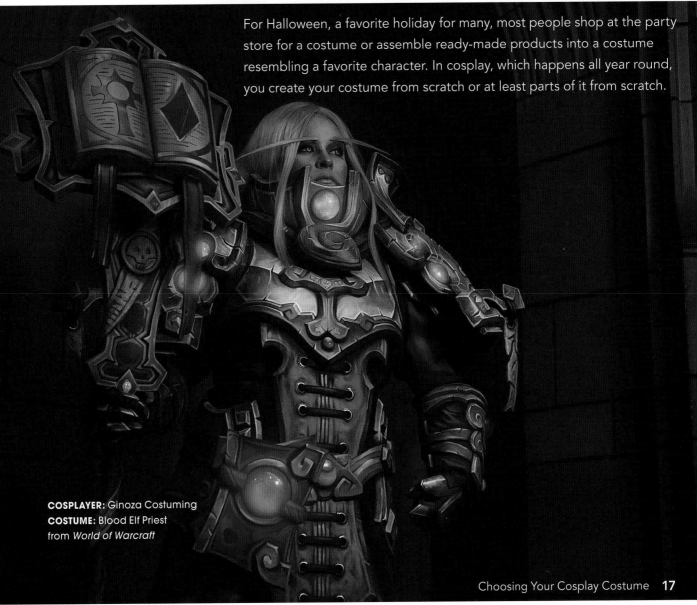

For Halloween, a favorite holiday for many, most people shop at the party store for a costume or assemble ready-made products into a costume resembling a favorite character. In cosplay, which happens all year round, you create your costume from scratch or at least parts of it from scratch.

COSPLAYER: Ginoza Costuming
COSTUME: Blood Elf Priest
from *World of Warcraft*

Now that you have decided you want to jump into cosplay, there is no more shopping at the party store. So where do you start?

LEFT TO RIGHT:
Jackie Craft, me, Mogchelle, BubblesGal0re

- **PREPARE MENTALLY.** Wearing a costume outside the month of October can take getting used to. People stare, ask what you are doing, and most of the time have absolutely no clue about what cosplay is. Sometimes explaining it to them is fun, but sometimes it's just best to say, "I'm heading to a comic book or video game convention." If you aren't ready for people to ask, stare, or even take photos, then maybe a trip to a convention before you cosplay is a good idea.

- **WATCH OTHER COSPLAYERS.** Watch (*not creepily!*) how they interact with different types of people. Cosplayers draw attention to ourselves when we are in costumes, and it's a great thing! Sometimes as a cosplayer at a convention, I wear many hats. I typically keep in character and act like my cosplay character so I don't "break the magic" for younger kids, especially with Disney characters. Other times I pose for a very long time in front of a lot of cameras. Local news or major companies, like Marvel and Star Wars social media teams, often interview me, too. These opportunities are the icing on the cake for me. It's an amazing feeling. However, it's totally okay to turn down those types of opportunities. No one is making you sit for interviews or even pose for a photo. You can say no, thank the requester, and move on. See Convention Time (page 101) for a more complete look at what it's like to be a cosplayer during a typical convention day.

- **RESEARCH.** Understanding what is involved in creating your chosen costume can help you avoid becoming overwhelmed. Take the time to do some research! There are so many resources (next page). Learn about the costume you want to make; a bit of preliminary guidance will give you a more realistic picture of the amount of time you will need to invest, how much it will realistically cost, and how to juggle your creative ideas with sewing skills so you end up with a successful costume.

Research

COSPLAYER: April Gloria
COSTUME: Character from *Fallout*

COSPLAYER: MirrorBright Cosplay
COSTUME: Thrawn from *Star Wars*

COSPLAYER: ToughTink
COSTUME: Pink Diamond from *Steven Universe*

START ON THE INTERNET

The most useful place to start is the internet. Start with a Google Image search using the name of the character you want to cosplay as the search term. Once you start typing, several suggested searches appear. For example, if you want to cosplay Captain Marvel, begin by opening your browser and typing "Captain Marvel costume."

Look through the images to become familiar with the costume. Try to see the costume from all angles. Take note of the components of the costume, the general look, any conspicuous lines, the colors used, and any other particularly noteworthy details.

Make a folder on your desktop for this costume and start saving images to this folder. The more images the better. Don't be afraid to pull images from behind the scenes or from fan or concept art. You want any and all images you can find so you can begin to develop a full-body view of the character.

Note: Fan Art

Fan art *is a short term for any kind of art created from a certain fandom as its subject matter done by artists both unofficial and official sanctioned by the intellectual property. Fan art is a large community on the internet and is found on websites like Tumblr and DeviantArt (see Resources, page 126).*

If you do find new and more modern images from these sites, it is important to try contacting the artist for permission for you to duplicate their work. Not all artists allow cosplayers to create their work. Most artists allow you to use their work as inspiration, or some might allow you to copy it into cosplay form.

COSPLAYER: Jedimanda
COSTUME: Captain Marvel from *Captain Marvel*

Grabbing Detail

Now that you have a good understanding of what your character's costume looks like, you'll need to locate higher-resolution images to pin down more specific details. These can really make or break your costume's authenticity. Higher-resolution images help you find small and intriguing details so you can plan your costume construction. A good-quality photo might help you determine if a costume is a full-body suit or separate pieces, and it helps you see tiny details such as seams, embroidery, paint gradations, closures, and weathering on armor.

Find higher-resolution images of your chosen costume by selecting the Tools option at the top of your search screen; a submenu bar will pop up. From this bar, select *Size* and then select *Large*.

To determine the actual size of an image, click on the image to open a preview screen. A size definition appears at the bottom of the image. Image size relates to the pixels in the image: The more pixels in an image, the higher the quality and the larger the image. This is specifically helpful if you want to enlarge the photo to see details and further expand your knowledge on how to make the garment.

Unfortunately, color is inconsistent throughout the web. Many photos of your character can be photoshopped to completely change the costume color—for a season, a publication, or personal preference. Be aware that any image you find online might not be the correct color. In addition, with different computers and mobile devices, brightness, contrast, and color shifting on the monitors can be an issue. Double-check your original source throughout your build to confirm and keep on track with your specific color scheme. I know from experience that the magazine *Entertainment Weekly* loves to take liberty with color on their covers!

SCREENSHOTS: BEYOND THE BASIC SEARCH

Now that you have found your way around Google, it's time to expand your research. Before we talk about different websites to gather further imagery, let's go old school and grab a camera and tripod. Set up the movie, video game, or television show that features your character and photograph your character from the screen. Pause, snap, pause, snap, pause … and keep snapping! This is called *screenshotting*, and having these photos of your character is one of your best research options. Most of time, the character's garment is shown in the best light on screen, allowing you to see its true color. The screenshots will (hopefully) give you multiple angles of your character. Don't be afraid to take lots of photographs, but keep in mind you are photographing in higher resolution. This is good because it allows you to zoom in and check out those small details that you want to know about. Photoshop or a simple photo-viewing application allows you to zoom in and out to see details from close up and far away. This is ideal when deciding how to plan the details of your costume.

PINTEREST: A VIRTUAL MOOD BOARD

Pinterest is a consistently running social media image feed. You can follow other people's accounts, and just like with other social media, when an account you follow adds a new pin, it appears on your news feed. When you pin things to your Pinterest account, Pinterest adds associated pins to whatever content you are researching in your news feed. This is ideal and is one of the main reasons I love this format. The other main reason is the option to form *boards*.

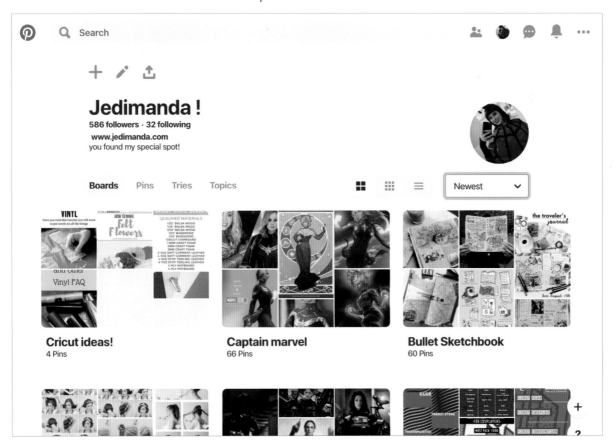

How to Form a Board

1. Go to your profile, click the plus sign in the upper left corner, and choose *Create board*.

2. From here, decide on the name of your board and choose your visibility preference. You can opt to keep it public, which means everyone can see what you pin, or you can choose to keep it a secret, or private, board. This means that no one can follow you and anyone that searches for you cannot view this board. This is a great option for those super-secret surprise cosplays you are building for your next convention.

3. Now it's time to fill your board! Fill your board by searching for images within the website and clicking *Save*. Save the images to the appropriate board (assuming you have developed several boards with different themes).

4. Your boards are a great place to upload and share your recent film screenshots I spoke about earlier. Now, instead of choosing *Create board* choose *Create pin*. This opens a new screen where you can upload and define a pin. Drop in your photo to upload it to your board, and give your pin a title and an optional short description. Select the board to pin it to and click *Save*.

Congratulations—
you've started your virtual mood board! Now go off and pin to your heart's content. One bonus about Pinterest is that you can download the Pinterest app and have your boards with you on the go! Pin at home on your desktop, head to a craft store, and pull up your inspiration pins on your mobile phone as you shop.

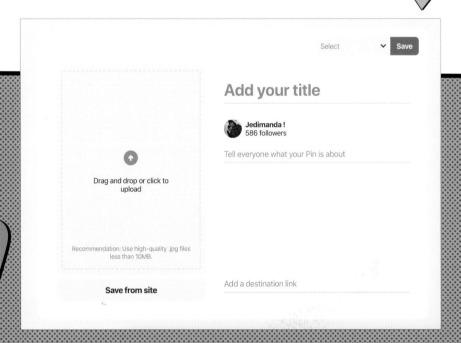

INSTAGRAM

Another useful social media to use for research is Instagram. Here you can find other cosplayers' versions of your character and how others interpreted your costume. It's a great place for communication and for reaching out to other crafters to see how they made their costume. This is where a lot of cosplayers find me and ask about costumes or pieces I've made.

Besides the general following, hashtags are key. A *hashtag* is a group of one or more words put together with the pound/hashtag symbol (#) before it. This is a common search tool within social media. Hashtags allow images to be attached to them and easily searched. Most social media users use hashtags to define the photo or video they are posting so

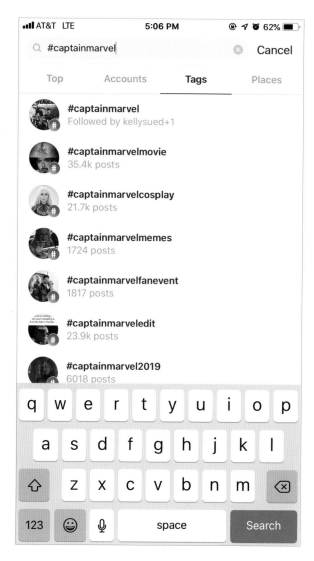

others may find them—easy to share, easy to find. Use this to your advantage. See how others made your character's outfit; view different images and art of your character. Like all search engines, make sure to double-check colors and tones. Sometimes you might stumble across a rare find.

Instead of doing the general hashtag search with the name of your character as the subject, try getting a little more defined. Put the words *cosplay* or *movie* at the end of your tag. For example, instead of just #CaptainMarvel, try #CaptainMarvelcosplay or #CaptainMarvelmovie. Sometimes those populate different results that could help with your cosplay plan. Get creative with your hashtags and have fun searching with this mobile social media!

YOUTUBE

The final and crucial research site is YouTube. This is where you start to see not just costume images but also how people make their costumes. The videos may be long, but the information is key. They are inspirational, provide a guide to the work ahead, and even give you a sense of how much time you might need to invest in making your costume.

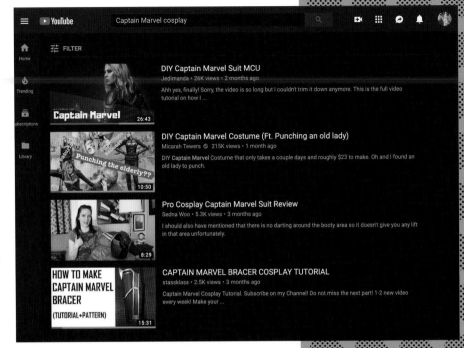

Many video creators love to share their work, and you can get very defined information from the videos. I know because I share most of my cosplay builds on YouTube so I can help viewers with their creative process. If you aren't familiar with YouTube, I insist you explore this amazing site. Establish a profile and save videos to playlists. Use the term *video tutorials* as a keyword to search for your costume. Sticking with the Captain Marvel example, search for *Captain Marvel video tutorial*.

DEEP KEYWORD SEARCHES

Now this is where you get specific. This is where you start to define your costume and the various pieces that come together to make the costume.

Particularly helpful keywords in an internet search include crafting, DIY costume, patterning, armor, prop making, foam-smith, special effects, wigs, and makeup. Using the Captain Marvel example, try searching for *Captain Marvel armor* or *Captain Marvel DIY costume* once you have some images and ideas to start with. Use these keyword search terms on all the previous search engines and social media.

Budgeting

Now that you have a vision for your costume, you need to get a sense of how much time and money it will take to create. Don't be afraid to make a budget and stick to it. Many cosplay creators can attest to this statement. It's so easy to get lost in all the fabric and foam, but if you don't stick to your budget, you might be stuck with an incomplete costume or no money in your bank account. Yikes! Budgeting is tough love sometimes, and cosplay is pricey. I'm going to be upfront about that. But it's my main hobby, and it's what I love to do and how I like to spend my money. Being inspired to make a costume is great, but it is important that real life comes first. Please pay your rent instead of buying another bolt of silk (even though that is tempting)! Be honest with yourself and your money.

Ball gowns, big armor builds, and heavy special effect makeup can be costly. I've spent over $500 United States Dollars on materials for costumes—my Anastasia ball gown to be exact. But I budgeted for it, since I knew the silks I chose would be pricey and the rhinestones I would purchase to have the gown shine like a diamond would expensive. It's what I wanted, and I made it happen without sinking myself into an ocean of debt.

Don't be afraid to buy that expensive silk, but also don't be afraid to experiment and get creative with cheaper materials to achieve your look. It's all about what you put into your cosplay. You aren't being judged (unless you are competing—more on that later), and you aren't turning in your receipts. Be bold, experiment, and find ways to make your cosplay fit your budget.

ESTIMATING COSTS

Determine how much you want (and can afford) to spend and then begin the cost research. Start by making a list of all the various components of your costume. This includes *everything*. List the main clothing components (such as suits, pants, capes, cloaks, tops), accessories (belts, gauntlets, greaves, jewelry), footwear, armor, props, wigs, and anything else your costume includes.

Next, list the "ingredients" of each piece, just like for a recipe. For example, the top of my Captain Marvel costume required a sewing pattern, fabric, closures, specialty trim, and paint.

Once you have the list of ingredients, assign approximate costs for each item. I do this by checking prices on amazon.com and online, or in Jo-Ann Fabric and Craft Stores. I usually purchase the bulk of my supplies at Jo-Ann's, so searching their website (see Resources, page 126) for sale prices on items I know I need is helpful.

Sometimes Amazon can offer a better deal on notions (zippers, thread, buttons, snaps, needles, and pins), and I will buy through the Amazon website to stock up, but I do like to head to the Jo-Ann store where I can shop in person, feel the fabrics, and see the colors.

CM Top/Bodice ingredients
- sewing pattern
        - $2 (sale), retail ($25)
- fabric
        - $14.99 a yard, need 1 yard blue, 1 yard red,1 yard gold.
- thread
        - $3.50 a spool, need 3 colors
- interfacing
        - $7 a yard, need 3
- paint
        - $2 a tube, need 3 colors
- closures (zippers & snaps)
        - $7 zipper
        - $10 in various sized closures
- speciality trims (piping)
        - $7 a yard, need 3

ESTIMATING TIME

You've established your budget and costume costs, so here is the last piece of the puzzle: how to estimate your time commitment. Give yourself a deadline—a convention, a photo shoot, or even Halloween. Making a deadline gives you a goal for the build beyond simply finishing it. Pushing yourself and avoiding procrastination is half the battle when making a costume. Truly, it is.

Be realistic in estimating your own sewing skills and creative mindset. Are you a new sewist? If so, set aside time to learn and practice before jumping into creating your costume pieces. Don't be afraid to be a beginner. If you decide to create everything from scratch and this is your first cosplay build, choose a section or part of the build to practice and be prepared for mistakes—they happen! Typically, skirts are the easiest parts to build. If you plan to build both a skirt and a bodice, try building the skirt first and see how fast you move through it.

Creating a timeline for your project is essential. One of my costume builds, Queen Amidala's senate gown from *Star Wars: Episode I—The Phantom Menace*, took me nine months to build. The headpiece alone took me four months because I just couldn't grasp the build. I struggled and I procrastinated. It took two rounds of building that headpiece before I was finally finished it. Then the robe, tunic, and skirt took the remaining five months. However, I still met my deadline, Star Wars Celebration 2017. It was a tough build, but if I hadn't set that deadline and paid attention to it, I wouldn't have finished. The moral of the story is *set that deadline*!

TIP

Con crunch is a thing! It happens to a lot of cosplayers a month before their chosen show. People don't set their timeline and life can get in the way, but it's okay. However, rushing to complete an outfit is not fun and can totally ruin the experience and even affect your health. Don't let con crunch get you. If it does, ask for help from a friend or maybe purchase some pieces of your outfit. Cosplay isn't supposed to be stressful!

Making Versus Buying

Here is a common thought that a lot of cosplayers have: *If I don't want to make this, can I still cosplay?* I say, yes, absolutely! It's okay to buy pieces or even the whole outfit. I've purchased several pieces for my builds including leggings, wigs, shoes, belts, and even undergarments. Purchasing these items can help you push through your timeline even faster.

This book focuses on choosing a cosplay project and making it; however, I must include a branch of the cosplay world called *closet cosplay*. Closet cosplay is when players purchase or assemble the majority of the outfit with already created garments or props. Many people start cosplaying this way just to get the feel of the world. It's a good way to start, and you might even consider it the first step of the research process.

If you would like to purchase some pieces for your build, check your local secondhand stores as well as Amazon, Etsy, and eBay (see Resources, page 126). I've pulled many items from these places. It's fun to find vintage looks for certain eras for multiple fandoms. I know several people who love pulling vintage items for fun Doctor Who cosplays. You can visit sites that offer full costume sets like miccostumes.com and ProCosplay (see Resources, page 126). There are also dozens of artists on Etsy that can create multiple pieces at a commission price. Ask around, and you will find someone to help you. People can get super creative without creating a single item from scratch.

GETTING STARTED

Sewing is an art form (some people call it a craft, but I prefer art form) that involves stitching together elements with a needle and thread. The amount of stitching (fabric, trim, and notions) and how it's stitched together is up to the creator. Sewing is such a greatly variable art form, from fine arts to garment making and even to textile arts.

Ever since humans have worn clothing, they have been stitching clothing together, first by hand and then by machine with the invention of the sewing machine in the nineteenth century. It's the one thing all humans on this planet have in common: Every day we get dressed. Clothing in most societies is a requirement, so garment makers are necessary; their work is important. I worked as a tailor during my college years, stitching pant hems for workers and altering necklines for brides. I loved it—all of it! I loved the happy moment when I saw clients delighted with fixed and better-fitting clothing. It was then that I knew this tailoring gig was more than just a job; I was helping people achieve a level of happiness.

Once you learn to sew, you can really make anything. Every garment you see in a department store or online you can figure out how to make; however, learning the basics is the first step. Read on!

Sewing Tools

In my opinion, sewing is the starting point of costume creation. I think that cosplayers should have a basic knowledge of sewing. Aside from armor making, if you want to create a costume, you need to know how to put it together. That's where sewing comes into play. I've been sewing for over ten years now, and I feel like I have a good grip on sewing knowledge. This is where I shine, and I hope I can help you shine here as well.

There are so many cool sewing tools that make sewing easier, and you don't have to buy them all at once. You can start with an assortment of hand-sewing needles, thread, scissors, a ruler, a measuring tape, and fabric. Add to your sewing box as you become more involved with cosplay.

COSPLAYER: April Gloria
COSTUME: Elf from *Skyrim*
Photo by Casey Greseth

HAND-SEWING TOOLS

HAND-SEWING NEEDLES come in various lengths, sharpnesses, and eye sizes. (The needle *eye* is the name for the tiny hole at the top where the thread is pulled through.)

THREAD comes in different weights, colors, and fibers (such as polyester, nylon, cotton, and silk). I recommend grabbing some basic primary colors in cotton thread, especially black and white. Thread can be hidden in the seams or be part of the design.

A **THIMBLE** is a tiny metal cup you place over one of your fingers to help move the needle through the fabric. I highly suggest becoming comfortable using a thimble. I wear mine on my right middle finger and use that finger to help push the needle through heavy or textured fabrics. There is no right or wrong way to use a thimble, but it's a great hand tool to have in your sewing box.

BEESWAX, SEWING WAX, OR THREAD WAX—regardless of the name, this stuff is great for hand sewing. Running your thread through wax before you start stitching helps the thread stay straight and tangle free.

TIP

HOW TO USE BEESWAX
Thread your needle and place the thread on top of the wax. Press the thread down on the wax with one finger. With the other hand, pull the needle and thread between your finger and the wax. You can also heat-set the wax on the thread by running the thread under an iron before starting to stitch.

A **PINCUSHION** keeps all your needles and pins together and off the floor. I personally like the tomato-shaped ones because of the history behind them. During the Victorian era, it was customary for guests to bring tomatoes to new homeowners.

Placing tomatoes on the mantel was supposed to help repel bad spirits and boost prosperity for the house and its owners. Since tomatoes weren't always in season, guests would sometimes gift a small ball of red fabric filled with sand or sawdust. Over time, this item became a common place to put sewing pins and needles. As for the attached strawberry, it is usually filled with emery so you can clean and sharpen your needles by pricking it.

A **SMALL PAIR OF SCISSORS OR SNIPS** (often 4″) is essential for every sewing box. Refer to Cutting Tools (page 37) for more information about scissors. My favorite pair are the small black ones from Gingher.

You'll also need a **SEWING BOX** to keep your supplies organized and together. Any kind of box will do. I suggest a hard-sided box instead of a bag, but anything will work when you are getting started. Mine is my great-grandmother's purse. She was a seamstress like me, so this helps me keep a bit of her with me all the time.

TIP

You don't really need a needle threader, but it sure is helpful. Sometimes the eye of the needle is super tiny and tough to see. You can thread your needle by inserting the pointed loop through the eye of the needle, inserting your thread through that loop, and pulling the threader back out through the eye. Voilà! You can even use this to help thread your sewing machine, too.

HAND-SEWING STITCHES

The **running stitch** is the most commonly used stitch. It is a series of short, evenly spaced straight stitches. The shorter the stitch length, the stronger the stitch. The longer the stitch length, the looser the stitch. Long running stitches are often referred to as *basting stitches* and are used to temporarily hold fabrics or trims together.

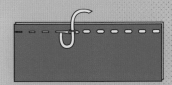

Running Stitch

The **backstitch**, like the running stitch, is a popular hand stitch. It is most often used for seaming because it is so strong. There are no spaces between the stitches. Start with a single running stitch (usually ¼″ long). Bring the needle up through the fabric a stitch length away; then stitch backwards into same (closest) hole of the previous stitch. Continue with this motion.

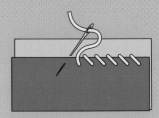

Backstitch

TIP

Machine backstitching is also called *back tacking* and should be done at the beginning and end of most seams so the seam doesn't open.

Whipstitches are quick to form and are used often to hem fabric edges. They are formed with a series of same-size diagonal stitches that wrap around the edge of the fabric.

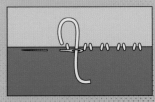

Whipstitch

Blind stitches create an invisible seam and are used mostly on lighter fabrics to give a seamless look. This stitch is often used to hem and involves folding the fabric so the stitches are hidden in the fabric fold.

Blind stitch

Styling Design
Ruler
Dritz

Armhole Curve Use 13–26

Hip Curve Use 1–17

WESTCOTT

STAINLESS STEEL

MEASURING TOOLS

Making clothing requires more than just your usual 12″ ruler. I recommend having a couple of measuring tools on hand at all times. Most rulers serve multiple functions for measuring and marking, as well as aiding in pattern making. A few of the rulers listed below are all you need:

- A flexible 2″ × 18″ plastic ruler allows you to mark seam allowances as well as view the fabric underneath. A small 1″ × 6″ ruler is handy for marking seam allowances on the fabric edge and for any other small measurements.

- A slightly larger and sturdier ruler for all kinds of marking. They are available in many sizes and shapes.

- A French curve ruler is more for pattern drafting but can also be used for measuring and marking curves.

- Cheap and handy! Yardsticks are ideal to have around because most sewing and quilting rulers are 18″ or 24″ long, whereas a yardstick is 36″ long. Yardsticks are useful for measuring wide widths of fabric.

- You must have a tape measure (or measure tape) for body measuring because it can wrap around the body to give the most accurate measurement. It also is longer than a ruler.

CUTTING TOOLS

You'll definitely need to cut your fabric at some point, and having an army of cutting tools is useful. Both scissors and rotary blades need to be the sharpest they can be. This means that you should only use your fabric scissors to cut fabric; when you use fabric scissors on something like paper, they dull quickly. Trying to cut fabric with dull scissors or blades can be tragic to your fabric. So, to help keep your fabric scissors identifiable, I recommend tying a piece of fabric or ribbon to the handle of your scissors and rotary cutter to mark them as "fabric only."

There are several different types of scissors, each specific to certain tasks.

DRESSMAKER'S SCISSORS or **STANDARD FABRIC SCISSORS** are the first type of scissors you'll want to buy. They are long-bladed scissors capable of cutting big lengths of fabric. They have tapered ends so they don't poke through the fabric or snag fabric fibers. These guys are heavy duty, so keep them in good shape.

CRAFT SCISSORS are what I call any other scissors that aren't going to cut fabric. Many brands feature cheaper, plastic handles. I would have about two or three pairs of these on hand because you end up cutting a lot of non-fabrics with cosplay costume making.

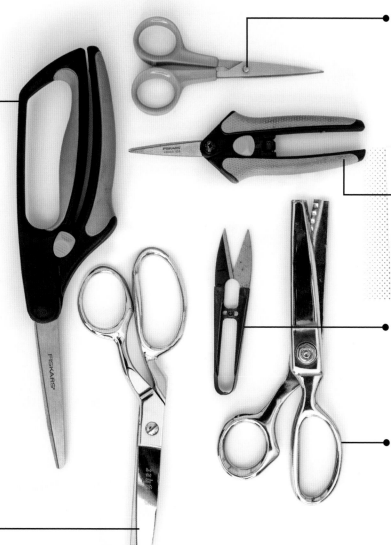

> **TIP**
>
> I don't personally own a pair of these, but *spring-loaded scissors* are handy for creators who have any type of hand issues like arthritis or general fatigue. Instead of using your hand muscles to open and close your scissors, the scissors themselves do half the work!

As discussed in Hand-Sewing Tools (page 34), **SNIPS** are ideal for many reasons. I mostly use them for snipping threads. These can also be used for appliqué and embroidery trimming.

PINKING SHEARS are a great because many fabrics fray and shred like crazy. Cutting with these shears helps slow the fraying. They don't completely prevent fabrics from fraying, but they do minimize the problem so you are better able to work with the fabric.

A **ROTARY CUTTER** uses a circular blade to cut with ease as the blade glides through the fabric. It is easy to cut curves by following the edge of curved pattern pieces, and you can also cut through multiple layers of fabric if the blade is large enough. There are different-size blades, and they can be sharpened. Rotary cutters have locking mechanisms to prevent accidental cuts. You need a **SELF-HEALING MAT** when using a rotary cutter to protect your table or cutting surface. The self-healing mat bounces back into shape once you run the rotary cutter over it, so you can use it multiple times. These mats will last a long time.

You will need an acrylic rotary ruler to use with a rotary cutter and mat.

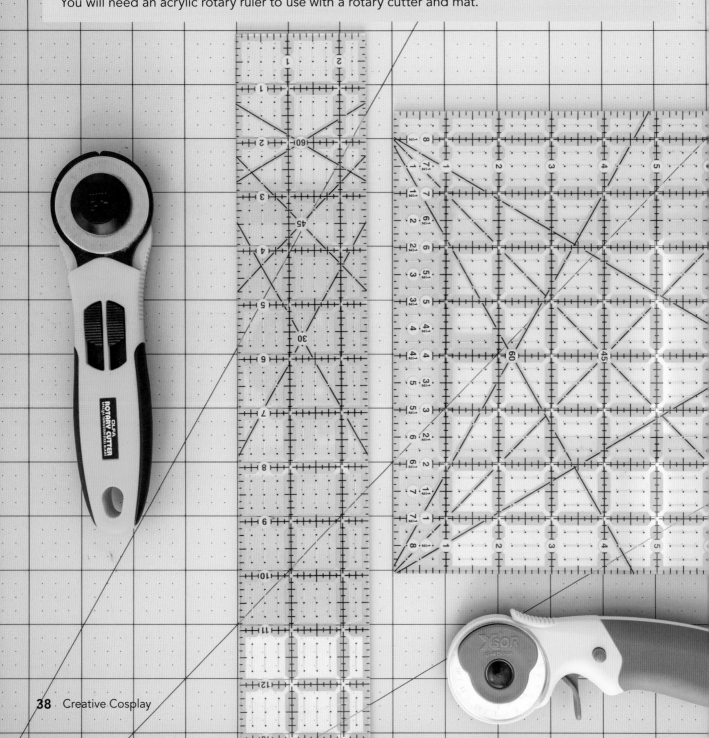

THE SEWING MACHINE

Now is the time to chat about the most important tool in your sewing studio: the sewing machine. Among all the tools you need, this is the most important and most substantial purchase. For ease and speed, you'll want to do most of your sewing with a sewing machine, though you can create garments with hand-sewing tools. Hand-sewing takes much longer and requires a lot of practice to get the stitches right so your costumes don't fall apart.

But what is a sewing machine? A sewing machine is used to sew pieces of fabrics or related materials together with thread. The machine itself is complicated, even though it performs a pretty basic function. If you are considering buying a sewing machine, I recommend BERNINA, Brother, Husqvarna Viking, Janome, JUKI, Pfaff, or Singer brand sewing machines. These are common brands in the United States and internationally.

HISTORY OF THE SEWING MACHINE

The history of the sewing machine dates to the mid-eighteenth century, with many people working to create and finalize their own patent. Everyone's brain waves were working at the same time to try and make this machine work; different people were creating different types of machines, and the various machines were forming a variety of different stitches. In 1846, Elias Howe invented a machine that most closely resembles sewing machines today. However, it was Isaac Merritt Singer who successfully marketed the sewing machine, allowing him to pay substantial judgments for patent infringement. Singer sewing machines are some of the most purchased machines in history. In short, sewing machines have a long history of patent backstabbing and courtroom arguments!

Sewing Machine Basics

Let's chat about the sewing machine, and I'll try to provide a basic understanding about how it functions. Every sewing machine is different, which is why the instruction manual that comes with your machine is key. But basically, they all sew the same—a top (needle) thread interlocks with a bottom (bobbin) thread to form the stitch.

To start:

- Locate the on and off switch and plug in the machine.

- Examine your machine. Find the button or foot pedal that starts the sewing action.

- Determine if you have a front-loading or top-loading bobbin. Wind a bobbin and insert it into the machine. (Refer to the owner's manual—loading the bobbin correctly is important.)

- Refer to the owner's manual to thread your machine. There are often color-coded thread paths on many machines. Take care and make sure the machine is properly threaded or the stitches won't look or behave correctly.

- Look at your machine and locate the dials or buttons that identify the stitch type, width, and length. These are important because they are how you tell the machine what and how to stitch.

Sewing Machine Stitches

There are so many different sewing machines! Some computerized models can sew over 100 stitch variations. Honestly though, costume making really only requires the straight stitch, zigzag stitch, backtack (reverse) stitch, blind hem, overlock stitch, and buttonhole stitch. Even the blind hem, overlock, and buttonhole stitches are optional (although fairly standard on most machines and really nice to have).

TIP

Listen to your machine. It will sound differently if is something is amiss with the mechanics. If something doesn't sound right, stop sewing and rethread the needle and reinsert the bobbin. Most of the time, rethreading will take care of the strange sounds. You should also refer to your owner's manual for a maintenance schedule.

THE SERGER

A serger is a great addition to a sewing room, but it's not necessary at the beginning of your cosplay journey. Eventually you will want to invest in this wonderful machine. A serger is an overlocking machine that trims and clean finishes fabric edges to prevent them from fraying, all in one step. The serger also makes seams that stretch without the thread breaking. Most sergers stitch with 3–5 threads. The more threads, the greater the variety of stitches. All you really need when just starting out is a 3-thread serger that can trim seam allowances, overlock/clean finish the fabric edge in one pass, and stitch together high-stretch materials. You will love it!

Safety Tips

- Watch your fingers!

- If you have long hair, pull your hair back into a clip or elastic.

- Unplug your machine when you aren't using it. You might even want to cover it with a fabric scrap to keep the dust off (unless you are so hooked you sew all the time).

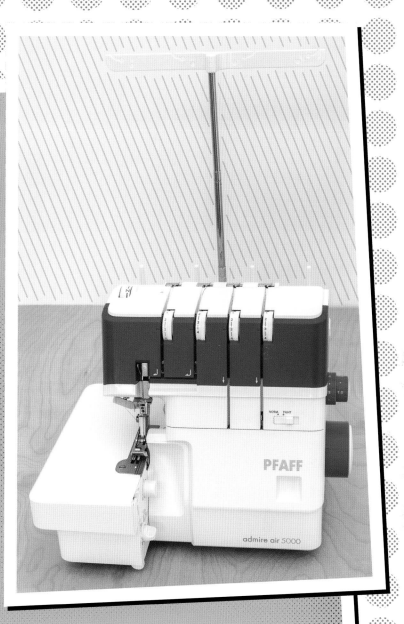

Fabrics

Fabric is a vast and exciting topic. Before hopping to your nearest fabric store, you'll want to understand a bit about fabric. It can be daunting just looking at all the aisles stocked full of bolts upon bolts of fabric. I find it extremely therapeutic to stroll down those aisles and feel all the different textures. I've gotten to the point now where I can understand how fabrics will look and feel by just touching them. This skill comes with time and knowledge. Read on so you can learn how to choose fabrics wisely for yourself and your project.

WHAT IS FABRIC?

Fabric is a textile (cloth) made up of yarns (yarn is multiple strands of thread spun together) that has been woven or knitted together. Some of the first clothing was created from animal skins to help keep early humans warm. As time progressed, humans began developing and experimenting with different materials to weave together into fabric.

Fabric Sources

Today, fabric is commonly created from four different sources: animals, plants, minerals, and synthetics. Fibers gathered from these sources are made into fabrics.

- **ANIMAL FIBERS** include wool from sheep, silk from silkworms, and fur and leather from a variety of animals. Animal-based fabrics can be expensive but worth the price in many cases.

- **PLANT FIBERS** include predominately cotton, bamboo, flax, and hemp. Plant-based fabrics aren't as expensive as animal-based fabrics because of the abundance of plants and the ease of production; they are usually the most available type of fabrics sold in fabric stores. Most consumer-sold fabrics contain plant fibers (like cotton) mixed with synthetic fibers (like polyester).

- **SYNTHETIC FIBERS**, like polyester, are manufactured and not created in nature. Many synthetic materials, including nylon, acrylic, and spandex, are used to create fabric. Rayon is a man-made fiber from natural sources.

- **MINERAL-BASED FIBERS** are made from mineral materials like asbestos and glass. Textiles made from these textiles are not necessarily used for making clothing. Fiberglass and vinyl tiles, as well as large theater curtains, were made with these materials. Asbestos is no longer used to make curtains because of its links to cancer.

FABRIC PRODUCTION

Now that you understand fibers, let's talk about how fibers become fabric in the production process.

Wovens

Most fabrics are woven, as it is the most common and fastest way to make textiles. There are several ways to weave fabrics, and it is the angles at which the fibers are woven that produces different fabrics. Most fabrics are woven at right angles on a loom. A *loom* is the machine, mostly mechanized in today's world, that creates textiles. Woven fabrics are good for making structured garments.

Denim, flannel, and muslin are good choices for heavily-tailored garments. Lighter-weight woven fabrics like chiffon and organza are also popular choices for less-tailored costumes. The majority of your first builds will probably be with woven fabrics.

Knits

Knit fabrics are constructed by the interlocking of fibers. Instead of being woven, imagine loops with the fibers pulled through. Knitting allows the fabric to move and stretch but also bounce back into place. If you are making garments that have a drape and flow to their look, or that will need to stretch, you'll want to use a knit fabric.

Nonwovens

Nonwoven fabrics are created by melting, bonding, and felting fibers together. These fabrics include faux leather and felt, and can be strong and hold the weight of heavy trims and novelty accessories well. They are good for making accessories.

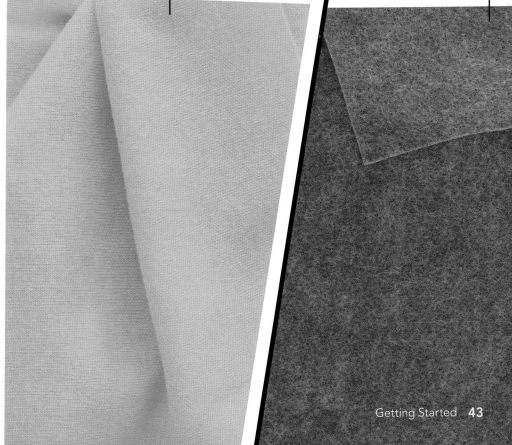

TYPES OF FABRICS

Once you understand how fabric is made, it is easier to understand the fabric itself and how it behaves. Once you really start to dive deep into fiber contents and fabric textures, you will find yourself understanding why pattern envelopes suggest the fabrics they do. This a pretty powerful skill set in the art of cosplay.

Satin, cotton blends, flannel, crepe back satin, and jersey knits are just the tip of the iceberg for the types of fabrics used in cosplay. With hundreds of fabric types to choose from, here the ones that I believe are the most useful for cosplayers. This isn't a finite list, but it's a good start.

Brocade

Brocade is a rich, heavy, and luxe fabric. Use this fabric for all your royal cosplays. The root word for brocade is *broccato*, which is Italian for "embossed cloth." Brocades have been woven on a loom for centuries for the finest of folks. Brocade is heavily decorated, sporting outdoor scenes with birds and leaves, paisleys, damask, and all sorts of designs. Just like lace, brocade weaving is an art form, so the fabrics can be expensive. Consider hand sewing beads and sequins onto brocade to really make this fabric sing! This fabric does fray, so be sure to finish the edges before you start sewing.

COSPLAYER: Jedimanda
COSTUME: Cersei Lannister from *Game of Thrones*

Chiffon

Chiffon is a popular fabric because of its light weight and sheer quality; however, it is also one of the most difficult fabrics to work with because it doesn't stay still. As soon as you cut chiffon, it starts to fray—so be careful and plan exactly what you need to sew. Handle the pieces carefully. You might even want to overlock stitch the cut edges or pink them with pinking shears to prevent the massive fraying. To keep the chiffon from shifting while you are sewing, pin the pieces together with a lot of pins. The fabric layers will shift unless if you pin every ¼″ or so. Make sure you remove the pins before your fabric goes under the sewing machine presser foot. If you are still having issues sewing chiffon, try using a walking foot on your sewing machine.

COSPLAYER: Jedimanda
COSTUME: Mary Poppins from *Mary Poppins*

Chiffon adds a level of elegance to anything, and its uses are endless. I like to pair chiffon with organza. Chiffon is most often found in 100% silk, 100% polyester, and a blend of silk and polyester.

Dupioni

Dupioni is one of my absolute favorite silk fabrics, although it can also be made with rayon and polyester fibers. I use silk dupioni for many of my builds because I love its look and feel. Dupioni is characterized by its knobby, three-dimensional texture, plain weave, and visible grain. *Grain*, short for *grainline*, refers to the way the fabric is woven together. When dupioni is woven with two different-color silk threads, it has a two-tone shine in different lights, which is really beautiful. The uneven, nubby texture also makes it a standout fabric, popular for formal wear and corsetry.

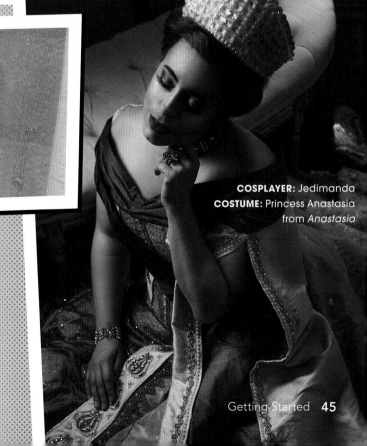

COSPLAYER: Jedimanda
COSTUME: Princess Anastasia from *Anastasia*

Felt

Felt is a nonwoven fabric that's created by pressing together fibers. It's great for making hats and sometimes shoes. I use felt as a stabilizer to reinforce some fabrics, but I wouldn't necessarily recommend it for making garments. If you are recreating an authentic 1950s poodle skirt, then definitely go for the felt!

Jersey

Jersey is a knit fabric. The interlocking construction method allows the fabric to move, stretch, and bounce back to its original shape. Jersey knit, or jersey for short, is made from a variety of different fibers, including wool, cotton, polyester, and acrylic. It is a great fabric for simple garments like causal dresses, skirts, and T-shirts: the items you'd want to make as foundation pieces for your cosplays. Jersey feels good against the skin. It also can be knitted with different interlocking processes to make lightweight and thin knits or stiff and heavy knit fabrics. You might want to spend some time in the fabric store becoming familiar with the different types of knit fabrics like single knits, double knits, and interlock jersey.

COSPLAYER: Jedimanda
COSTUME: Ahsoka Tano from *Star Wars Rebels*

Lace

Lace comes in a variety of colors, patterns, weights, designs, and fibers (silk, cotton, polyester, and even metallic fibers). It is like tulle, but the "holes" are arranged in beautifully decorative patterns. Use lace to add a luxurious note to your costume, either as yardage or in the form of trim. Keep in mind that lace is delicate and does require some special sewing techniques.

Leather

Leather is a flexible and durable fabric. Many people use this animal-based material for jackets, boots, belts, corsets, and accessories. If you are looking for a nonanimal-based fabric product similar to leather, try vinyl and/or Ultrasuede.

Leather can be painted with specific leather paints as well as tooled for details.

COSPLAYER: Jedimanda
COSTUME: Queen Amidala from *Star Wars: Episode I— The Phantom Menace*

Leather does not fray and does not have a grain, so you can use the entire hide for your pattern pieces. Keep in mind when shopping for leather that shops do not give swatches and you cannot purchase by the yard. Typically, you have to purchase by the hide, meaning the entire animal skin. A great option for purchasing leather is recycled leather. Thrift and secondhand stores have plenty of leather jackets, pants, upholstery, belts, and accessories. Either undo, untie, seam rip, or cut apart all the leather you need from your recycled purchases. I do this often! Do not wash leather; spot clean only.

Synthetic leather is a less expensive option and perfectly suitable for many cosplays.

Linen

Linen, both a fiber and a fabric, is one of the oldest plain weave fabrics. It is created from flax fibers and is popular during warmer weather, because it stays comfortable even when the temperature soars. It's an ideal fabric for linings and undergarments, as well as outerwear and some daily wear clothes. Linen can be purchased in different weights and is easily dyed, making it vibrant in many colors.

COSPLAYER: Jedimanda
COSTUME: Doctor Strange
from *Doctor Strange*

Muslin

Muslin is a basic, inexpensive cotton fabric with a plain weave. It is not decorative and can be used to make practice costume pieces to help you determine if they will fit or match your vision. It's the ideal fabric for testing ideas and patterns for your garments. You could also use muslin for linings. This is a good fabric to always have on hand.

Organza

Like chiffon, organza is a lightweight sheer fabric. The main difference is that chiffon has a slightly heavier drape, while organza seems to be floating in the air. Organza, like chiffon, can be difficult to use; it, too, shifts during cutting, so be sure to weigh the fabric down when you cut it. You can use fabric weights or metal washers from the hardware store. I suggest using organza for petticoats and anything that needs a little fluff. It's a soft fabric that can poof your gowns just like tulle or netting petticoats but is much nicer against the skin. Organza is found in 100% silk, 100% polyester, or a polyester blend. Remember to finish your edges well because this fabric frays like crazy. If you are having difficulty sewing organza, I suggest using a walking foot on your sewing machine.

COSPLAYER: Jedimanda
COSTUME: Mary Poppins from *Mary Poppins*

Quilting Cotton

Quilting cotton, the printed fabric you see in bulk at craft stores, is 100% cotton. It tends to be used most often by quilters and not so much for cosplay, but the beautiful range of patterns and colors are fun, and I have used it for linings. Remember: If you use this fabric, prewash it before cutting it out because it tends to shrink.

Satin

Satin is a fabulous fabric, known for its shiny surface. Satin is used mostly for formal wear and accessories. I used it for many of my ball gowns. Be aware that there is a right and wrong side to this fabric, and it tends to fray easily. Pink the cut edges with pinking shears, or use a serger to finish the edges before cutting it. Use the fabric amount listed on the pattern envelope for fabrics with nap since all the pieces cut from satin must be placed in the same direction. Satin is made of silk, nylon, or polyester fibers and is available in a wide price range. This is a beautiful fabric to work with for many different types of garments.

COSPLAYER: Jedimanda
COSTUME: Wonder Woman
from *Wonder Woman*

COSPLAYER: Jedimanda
COSTUME: Queen Amidala
from *Star Wars: Episode I—The Phantom Menace*

Shantung

Like dupioni, shantung is a silk fabric but lighter in weight and less irregular. Shantung is often machine woven, making it less expensive than hand-woven dupioni fabrics. I use shantung when I need to purchase a large amount of silk fabric. Shantung is a good dupe for silk.

Spandex

Spandex is a popular cosplay fabric, particularly for superhero suits and anything that needs to stretch. Spandex is an anagram for the word *expands*. Spandex, a synthetic fiber fabric, is the term that is commonly used in North America, but in Europe and other parts of the world, they use the term Lycra to describe the same fabrics. Lycra is the brand name created by the company DuPont in 1958. When you are making skintight garments that need to hug the body, be sure to purchase four-way stretch spandex, which stretches in all four directions. Spandex is always four-way stretch, but sometimes in stores it's stocked near knit fabrics that are two-way stretch. While two-way stretch fabrics have their use, you do not want to use them for skin-tight garments. (You'll want to be able to sit down, right?) When stitching spandex fabric, make sure to use a ballpoint/stretch needle and sew with a zigzag stitch. Spandex is great for super suits, leggings, active wear, and anything tight fitting.

COSPLAYER: Jedimanda
COSTUME: Jean Grey from *X-Men*

Suede

Suede is great to use for corsetry and accessories like belts and pouches. It comes in different weights and at different price points. Suede is the soft underside of the animal skin, perfect for jackets and shoes or anything that needs some durability and texture. Take care when sewing suede because if you need to remove stitches, the holes remain. Suede is a spot-clean fabric, so don't throw it in the washer and dryer.

Suiting

Suiting fabrics are wool- or polyester-blend fabrics that are used for making suits, hence the name. I use suiting fabrics a lot to create tailored garments that need to breathe. Suiting comes in all colors and patterns and is often cheaper to use for experimenting with your design. I love to embroider directly onto the fabric, and the fabric holds appliqués well.

COSPLAYER: Jedimanda
COSTUME: Queenie Goldstein from *Fantastic Beasts: The Crimes of Grindelwald*

Taffeta

Taffeta is another fabric that is made with silk fibers; it also made of acetate, polyester, and fiber blends, which are beautiful too. This fabric is crisp, medium- to heavyweight, and perfect for structured garments. It is also easy to press. I love using taffeta for ball gowns. Several members of royalty wore gowns made of silk taffeta—just find portraits of Marie Antoinette and eighteenth-century French nobility, and you will see silk taffeta. Pure silk taffeta can cost you a pretty penny, so consider other fibers, particularly if your costume requires a lot of yardage.

Tulle Netting

Tulle, netting, or tutu fabric is the fabric with tiny holes that is super strong and can hold its own weight without drooping. It is often used to create tutus for ballerinas. You can use tulle by pleating or gathering it to add structure to gowns, making them puff out. Tulle is used in almost every gown I've seen that achieved the Cinderella level of puffiness. Use this fabric to make petticoats, or flatline it to the edges of a slip layer under a dress (see Sewing Terminology, page 70). Tulle usually doesn't need to be hemmed and comes in silk, polyester, and nylon fibers.

COSPLAYER: Jedimanda
COSTUME: Mary Poppins from *Mary Poppins*

Twill and Duck

Twill (also the name of a fabric weave) and duck are strong and somewhat stiff fabrics that can be used for many garments. They are typically made from 100% cotton, 100% polyester, or blends of the two fibers. Twill is suitable for corsets and linings, while duck, which often resembles canvas, is often used to create external pockets and accessories like tote bags. I use both fabrics to make flight suits, structured jackets, and capes. I love myself a good cape!

COSPLAYER: Jedimanda
COSTUME: Qira from *Solo: A Star Wars Story*

Ultrasuede

Ultrasuede is the fancier name for ultra-microfiber. It is used in place of real animal suede leather. I use Ultrasuede for corsets, belts, boots, and armor when leather isn't available or is too pricey. Don't wash Ultrasuede. Spot clean only.

COSPLAYER: Jedimanda
COSTUME: Rey from *Star Wars: Episode VIII—The Last Jedi*

Velvet

Velvet is a fun fabric for lush-textured builds. It is woven with tufted threads that are shaved down to give a super-soft texture. Velvet, just like other fabrics, can be created with natural and synthetic fibers. The natural-fiber velvets, like silk velvet, are more expensive than synthetic versions, but the synthetic velvets can give you the same look for half the price. Use velvet for coats, jackets, capes, and outerwear. Velvet is a napped fabric, and the pieces for a garment must all be cut in the same direction. For a similar look, use cotton velveteen, which is easier to sew.

COSPLAYER: Jedimanda
COSTUME: Queen Amidala from *Star Wars: Episode I— The Phantom Menace*

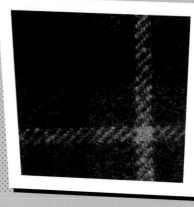

Vinyl

Vinyl is a diverse fabric that adds a plastic/ latex kind of industrial or leather look to any outfit. It does not fray when cut. Vinyl fabric can be stretchy and is often used in super suits. I use it for my suits as long as it has four-way stretch. Vinyl can be used as a replacement for leather fabric if you wish. It is a great fabric for experimentation!

Wool

Wool is a fabric that I must mention. I don't necessarily use it for a lot of cosplays because of the price and the unruliness it has with water and heat. However, wool can be great for outerwear and accessories like bags, pockets, satchels, and purses. The fabric cuts well and doesn't fray. Wool holds its shape and can be a great stabilizer for other fabrics. It tends to be bulky, so sew wool with a larger needle and a high-quality thread. Be careful when ironing wool because the fibers are easily scorched under high heat, and be sure to use the wool setting and a pressing cloth between the iron and fabric.

FABRIC TIPS

Learning about fabric is all about experimentation. Dye, trim, pleat, gather, and sew with a variety of fabrics to your heart's content. Consider fabric one of your best design tools!

- Stay away from the costume satin that appears in fabric stores before Halloween. This fabric is cheaply made and very difficult to work with. You might be tempted to try it because of its cheap price, but it frays like crazy, melts easily under an iron, and its super shine tends to look a bit cheap. Use it at your own risk!

- Take the time to prewash your fabric before you cut it. Unless you are using fabrics that obviously can't be washed, like silk, leather, or velvet, prewashing helps prep the fabric for sewing. You will particularly want to prewash cotton fabrics because they might shrink, and no one wants their garment to shrink after they make it. Prewashing also removes dyes that could bleed onto your skin or on light-colored fabrics that are also part of the costume, either while you are working with them or wearing them. See the Prewash column in Appendix A: Fabric Chart (page 123).

- Pay attention to the fabric fiber content if you are distressing the fabric by burning it. Cotton catches fire and will leave residue, whereas polyester will just melt, leaving a glued finished edge. Burning fabric could be harmful because of the fumes.

- Don't let expensive fabrics scare you. Make a mock-up (rough sample) first using muslin, cheap cotton, or cheap spandex, and save your money for the nicer fabrics once you have worked out the kinks and fitting issues in your design. Trust me—you will see a change in quality of your work once you use nicer fabrics. However, don't discount bargain fabrics! I use them all the time. I love getting creative with bargain-bin fabrics. I've created several cosplays with super-cheap quilting cotton, like my Wednesday Addams cosplay. Don't let a price scare you away from experimenting with all types of fabrics.

COSPLAYER: Jedimanda
COSTUME: Wednesday Addams from *The Addams Family*

Patterns

Now that you have determined what costume you want to make and have a basic knowledge of the sewing tools you need and the amazing variety of fabrics you can use, it's time to talk patterns. Unless you want to draft one yourself (which you can totally do!), you need to buy a pattern.

You can purchase patterns in a store or online. Craft stores like Jo-Ann, Michaels, Hobby Lobby, and even some Walmarts carry patterns. An internet search will provide you with several options for purchasing patterns online.

For beginner purposes, this book only covers store-bought patterns, where to find them, how to choose them, and how to use them. If you are interested in learning how to draft your own patterns, I suggest viewing YouTube tutorials and researching pattern making books. There is a definite learning curve to pattern making. You need to understand body shape and how to create the look of your cosplay.

WHAT'S A PATTERN?

A pattern is the beginning building block for all the parts of a garment, like the bodice front and back, sleeves, or pant legs. The pattern pieces are printed on paper. You use the paper pattern pieces to cut the fabric by pinning the pattern pieces to the fabric and cutting around the cutting lines, or tracing around them onto the fabric and cutting on the marked lines. Regardless, once you use the pattern pieces to cut the fabric, you are ready to sew those cut pieces into a garment. And you have the instruction sheet to show you how!

CHOOSING A PATTERN

Store-bought patterns have been around ever since Ebenezer Butterick created the first graded tissue-paper pattern back in 1863. Since then, home sewists have had an incredible variety of options. You can find a pattern for almost anything you want to make!

Sometimes, no matter how long you search, you just can't find the right pattern. Don't sacrifice your design because you can't find the perfect pattern. Instead, improvise by mashing together pattern pieces. I tend to do this a lot. First, I look for the shape I need, and then I see if garment parts can be substituted and switched between different patterns. For example, when making ball gowns, I often use the same pattern for the bodice but different sleeve pattern pieces from a range of other patterns (see Pattern Mash-Ups, page 72).

The Big Four

There are four major pattern brands: Simplicity, McCall's, Butterick, and Vogue Patterns. These are known as "The Big Four" in the sewing community. All these companies offer clothing patterns for all ages, genders, and sizes, from costumes to wedding gowns, doll dresses to men's suit jackets, bathing suits to pajamas, and even great accessories. Let's break down the differences between The Big Four.

MCCALL'S (my favorite brand) has patterns for men, women, and children and tends to offer the trendiest styles of today. They have the best costume/cosplay line of patterns in my opinion. Costumes designed by Yaya Han and Cosplay by McCall's are two collections that feature patterns for cosplayers. I've made several garments using them and I highly recommend them for your first cosplay creation. Other than those collections, McCall's also has a wide variety of modern looks from which to choose.

BUTTERICK is the oldest name in pattern making and offers patterns that are more traditional in style, as well as a great variety of historical patterns. I'm a big fan of their undergarment patterns. Shop here for more historical-based costume patterns.

VOGUE PATTERNS offers the most couture and avant-garde looks of today. These styles are hot off the runway and mostly cater to sewists wanting to create a dramatic look. Vogue Patterns does not offer a costume line but does have a lovely Vintage Vogue collection. Most of their patterns are on the medium to difficult side to create; however, Vogue Patterns offers a Very Easy Vogue collection that includes simple silhouettes and basic patterns for pattern mashing (page 72). I recommend giving this collection a look.

SIMPLICITY has several collections for a wide variety of looks for men, women, and children. Their costuming collection is as vast as McCall's and Butterick, with many patterns that feature popular costumes. Simplicity owns the brands Burda Style and New Look, which cater to very simple garment creation. Simplicity also offers official licensed patterns from companies like Disney—very helpful if you are trying to create accurate cosplays.

 TIP Patterns can be expensive, but they are often on sale. You can also look for coupons or hunt for sales at your local fabric store. Sign up for the emailing list of your favorite pattern store and you'll soon find coupons in your email.

INDIE PATTERNS OR BRANDS can usually be found on Etsy and eBay. They are mostly created by professional pattern drafters with specific garments in mind. Many of my friends (and I) have found specific indie patterns for period garments, cosplay-centered garments from video games, and anime costumes we know The Big Four won't carry. If you're searching for a certain look, try researching within costume-specific Facebook groups or blogs dedicated to that specific costume or genre. Most likely, an indie pattern is available.

WITH PATTERN IN HAND

With your pattern in hand, it's time to determine the correct size and choose the appropriate fabric and necessary notions. On the back of all pattern envelopes, there is a size chart, a list of suggested fabrics, and a table indicating how much fabric you'll need to make the entire garment. I recommend following the fabric suggestions as closely as possible, because the right type and weight of the fabrics you choose are important.

The envelope back also lists the notions, and even some of the embellishments, that you'll need to duplicate the photograph of the costume on the envelope front. Be sure to note what you'll need to close your garment, like buttons or zippers (see Closures, page 60), interfacing to support the garment, or even elastic.

COSPLAYER: Akakioga
COSTUME: Orisa Gijinka from *Overwatch*

Size

Compare your measurements to those on the back of the pattern envelope, as pattern sizing is often different from ready-to-wear sizing. Many patterns are sold with multiple sizes printed on the same pattern paper, perfect if your body is a winning combination of a few sizes (like me!). My measurements tend to vary within the pattern sizing, so I often use multiple sizes. Many patterns come in two different size-group options—sizes 6–14 or 14–22.

EASE

Ease refers to the amount of wearing and design ease that is built into a pattern. It is the amount of space between your body and the garment. Here is an approximate indication of the amount of ease in the following silhouette descriptions found on the pattern envelope. If you like your cosplays tight, you'll want a close-fitting pattern, and if you like a lot of room, go with a loose or very loose-fitting pattern. Just be aware that you will have to alter your garment to fit you almost 99 percent of the time. Store-bought patterns add a lot of ease, and nothing fits like a glove the first time around.

Silhouette	Tops	Bottoms
Close fitting	0″–3″	0″–2″
Fitted	3″–4″	2″–3″
Semifitted	4″–5″	3″–4″
Loose fitting	5″–8″	4″–6″
Very loose fitting	8″+	6″+

Closures

Closures, like zippers, snaps, and buttons, are the extra items you'll need to finish your garment. There are many types of closures, so let's chat about the ones you are most likely to use.

  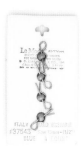

BUTTONS

Buttons are one of the oldest types of closures. They come in tons of different colors, shapes, sizes, and looks. There are two main types of buttons: sew-through and shank buttons. Sew-through buttons are flat, with either two or four holes, and they can be sewn directly to the garment. The shank button is typically used on suit jackets, pants, and delicate dresses and is characterized by the protruding loop on the back. Just like the sew-through buttons, shank buttons are easy to sew on garments—just in a different way. It's a good idea to create a thread shank, particularly for heavy buttons. Do this by anchoring your thread and running the thread through the button loop a few times, but leave the threads loose and let the button drape a little. Next, wrap the same thread around the loose threads to create the thread shank. This helps hold the button in place.

Sewing buttons in place is easy, but with every button comes a buttonhole. Most modern sewing machines have a separate foot attachment for making buttonholes and detailed instructions in the owner's manual. So never fear the buttonhole!

FASTENERS

Fasteners are a large group of closures including buckles, frogs, brooches, toggles, and D-rings. They are easy to hand sew in place. Some of my favorite fasteners are buckles and D-rings. These fasteners can also be dyed or painted to fit your needs.

GROMMETS AND EYELETS

Grommets and eyelets are great closures for any garment that need to be cinched in or let out to fit multiple sizes. Their purpose is to strengthen a tiny hole cut in the fabric so you can pull cording or ribbon through the hole, like a drawstring.

Grommets are two-part metal rings that sandwich a fabric hole. You need a special setting piece and a hammer to install a grommet. An *eyelet* is like a grommet except that it is one metal ring with an edge that can expand and grasp the fabric when you set it in with an eyelet-setting tool.

These closures are often used on ball gowns, corsets, and waist cinchers. They are a great option when you need some size flexibility. Paired with decorative cording or ribbon, these closures will quickly become your favorite.

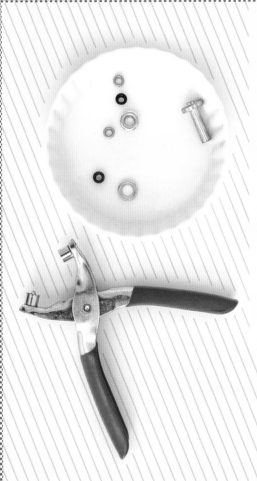

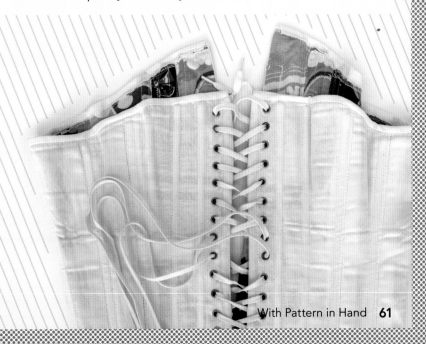

HOOK-AND-LOOP TAPE

Often called Velcro, this hook-and-loop fastener was created by Swiss engineer George de Mestral, in 1941. Available in different widths, lengths, and colors, it comes in two sections: One has little hooks and the other is fuzzy to catch the hooks. They can be sewn or glued onto fabric. I use hook-and-loop tape mostly for attaching heavy foam pieces onto my garments.

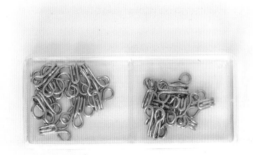

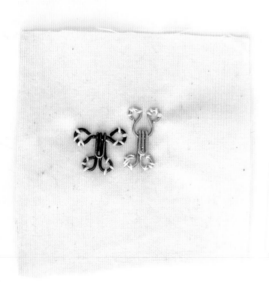

HOOKS, EYES, AND BARS

These guys are the handiest closures for sewists. They are metal wires formed into tiny hooks, bars, and eyes. *Bars* are straight pieces of wire with loops for sewing them down, and *eyes* are simple curved bars with loops for attaching them to fabric. These come in multiple sizes and in white, black, and silver finishes. Typically, when you install a zipper into a garment, there is a gap at the top where the zipper stops, but a hook and eye/bar combo finishes the closure completely. This is the most common closure combo in garments today.

MAGNETS

Magnets are fast becoming a popular closure. Depending on your garment, magnets can be the best closure because they don't damage the fabric. Some magnets come encased in plastic or fabric so you can sew them in place. You can sew a little fabric pocket for each of the magnets and insert them into hems, or topstitch the magnet fabric pocket to the fabric, and then boom—together! Magnets can also be glued in. They work great for attaching foam armor pieces to spandex suits.

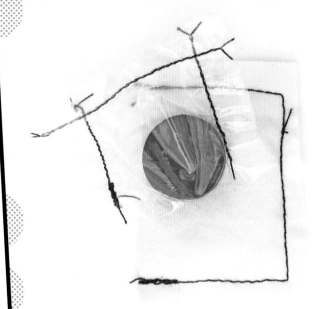

SNAPS

My second favorite closure—snaps! Snaps come in a variety of sizes and finishes, like gold, silver, and black. I mostly use sew-in snaps, but there are snaps that you rivet into place. Snaps are very handy for attaching items to a garment that you want to be able to remove. I purchase several different sizes; my favorites are size 10. I call them "Whooper Poppers!"

ZIPPERS

Zippers are one of the most popular garment closures. I use zippers in almost every costume I make. There are several different types in a variety of lengths, styles, and weights, including invisible, sport, heavy duty, separating, and coil zippers. I typically use polyester coil zippers. Your pattern envelope tells you what type of zipper to use and how long it should be, but its good idea to have a variety on hand. The invisible zipper does require a special sewing machine foot for installation, but the foot is inexpensive and readily available. Just pay attention to the directions printed inside the package to install it correctly. It takes patience and practice to install a zipper, but you can do it!

SHORTENING ZIPPERS

I often purchase the longest possible length of zippers in bulk because it is easy to adjust the zipper to the length I need. You can shorten all types of zippers except separating zippers, which need to be purchased at the exact recommended length.

1. Measure and mark the desired length by drawing a line with chalk right across the zipper teeth.

2. Machine stitch (very carefully) back and forth across the zipper tape and teeth to create a new zipper stop. I recommend turning the wheel by hand and avoid using the sewing machine foot pedal to maintain better control. This will prevent your needle from breaking.

3. Snip off the rest of the zipper about ½" beyond the new zipper stop.

Notions

Notions, also listed on the back of the pattern envelope, are the items necessary to complete the construction of your garment. These items are usually hidden inside a garment, though bias tape is used both functionally inside a garment and decoratively outside a garment.

BIAS TAPE

Bias tape is a flexible and non-fraying narrow fabric strip used to finish a garment edge and/or make piping. Varying in width from ½″ to 3″, bias tape is available in many colors and in single-fold and double-fold options. For single-fold bias tape, the raw edges have been folded inward and pressed. Double-fold bias tape is folded a second time over itself and pressed. It is good to keep a variety of bias tape packages on hand; you never know when you need to finish a troublesome armhole edge or fraying seam allowances. I use bias tape most often for binding the edges on bodices and corsets.

ELASTICS

Elastics allow your garments to stretch and hug your body. They come in various widths, shapes, and colors, and can double in length with full stretch. Be sure to check the pattern envelope to see if your garment calls for elastic. If it does, the envelope will indicate the necessary width and even the most suitable type of elastic.

You can sew elastic directly to fabric (use a ballpoint sewing machine needle and a zigzag stitch for maximum stretch) or insert it in a casing.

There are three types of elastic: braided, knit, and woven.

BRAIDED ELASTICS are ideal for swimwear, lingerie, sleeve hems, and leg openings.

KNITTED ELASTICS are soft and strong. They are the ones you will probably use most often in your costume creations. These elastics don't become narrower when you pull them to their fullest stretch and are easily sewn by hand or machine.

WOVEN ELASTICS are the strongest, but are typically used for upholstery and heavyweight projects.

INTERFACING

Interfacing is used to stiffen, strengthen, and stabilize knits or lightweight fabrics, or to achieve a special look. There are many interfacing weights, and you'll want to match the weight of the interfacing to your fabric. Check the information printed on the end of the interfacing bolt to see which fabrics are most suitable for that particular weight of interfacing.

There are two main types of interfacing, sew-in and fusible, and you can purchase both by the yard. Sew-in interfacing is typically used for fabrics that can't withstand high heat from an iron or for tailored garments. Fusible interfacing has adhesive on one side that adheres to the fabric with the application of heat and moisture. Refer to the instructions that come with fusible interfacing for fusing techniques.

Collars, jackets, sleeves, and bodices are just some examples of costume parts that might benefit from the addition of interfacing.

LINING

Patterns often call for lining. *Lining* is the innermost layer of fabric in a garment. Linings help conceal the seams, interfacing, padding, and sometimes mistakes! Linings help reduce the wear and tear of a garment, and they keep you warm. Depending on what you are making, you might be able leave out the lining, particularly since you won't be wearing your cosplay on a weekly basis. Refer to the back of the pattern envelope for more information and to Fabrics (page 42) to help determine suitable lining fabrics.

CREATING GARMENTS

Sewing cosplay costumes assumes some basic sewing know-how. If you have never sewn, you might want to take a sewing class or start by sewing a simple skirt or shirt. Sewing is a bit like riding a bike: Once you know how to sew, you can make anything and take it as fast or slow as you want!

In the same breath, know it's okay to make mistakes. All sewists make mistakes and learn from them.

Sewing Stitches

I'll guide you through sewing those all-important first stitches!

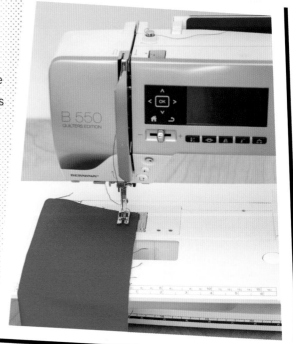

1. Lift the presser foot using the lever located around the back of the needle. This allows you to position the fabrics over the feed dogs, which move the fabrics along.

2. Position your fabric and lower the presser foot.

3. Look at the presser foot area. The metal plate that covers the bobbin is etched with several lines marked with numbers that act as seam allowance guides. You typically will sew with ¼″–⅝″ seam allowances. Keep your eyes on the guidelines (not on the fabric) to help you guide the edge of the fabrics as you stitch.

4. Locate your back tack, or reverse stitch, button. Press or activate the reverse stitch function when you begin and end the seam. This action prevents the stitches from coming out of your fabric and holds the ends of the seam together nice and tight.

5. Stitch at a comfortable speed. Most machines have a speed adjustment lever. Don't push or pull the fabric—let the feed dogs do their job and move the fabric for you. Be careful that you don't stitch over pins! You don't want to risk damaging your sewing machine or throwing off the timing.

And that's it—you just sewed. Give yourself a high five!

COSPLAYER: Pitchfork Cosplay
COSTUME: Ayesha from
Guardians of the Galaxy 2

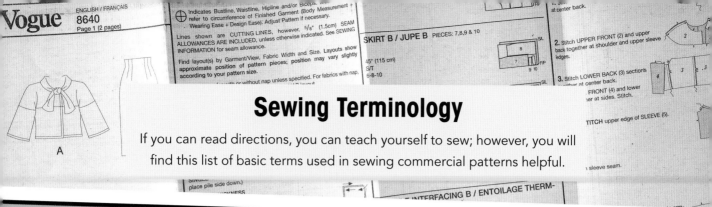

Sewing Terminology

If you can read directions, you can teach yourself to sew; however, you will find this list of basic terms used in sewing commercial patterns helpful.

FABRIC TERMS

BIAS The diagonal direction across the grain of woven fabric. Bias allows fabric to stretch.

GRAINLINE Fabric grainline refers to the orientation of the threads that make up the fabric. *Lengthwise grainline* is parallel to the selvage, *crosswise grainline* is perpendicular to the selvage, and *bias* is the 45° angle between the lengthwise and crosswise grainlines (which allows woven fabrics to stretch). There is a grainline arrow on all pattern pieces that helps you determine how to position the pattern on the fabric. Most pattern pieces are cut on the lengthwise grain. Position the pattern piece with the arrow parallel to the selvage. This is important so fabrics hang straight without strange wavering seams or hemlines.

RIGHT SIDE The "right" side of the fabric is meant to be shown; it is the decorative side. Sometimes it is hard to tell which side is meant to be the right side—so it's your choice! In sewing, the instructions will often tell you to sew two pieces of fabric with the right sides together.

WRONG SIDE The "wrong" side of the fabric faces the body. If a garment calls for interfacing (see Interfacing, page 67), you will apply the interfacing to the wrong side of the fabric. The wrong side of the fabric is also where you mark your pattern details and notches.

LINING TERMS

Patterns often call for lining. Refer to the pattern envelope and Fabrics (page 42) to determine the best lining choice for your project.

BAG LINING This is a method of lining jackets, outerwear, and accessories so that the lining is loose against the outer fabric. The lining seams and raw edges are hidden between the lining and the outside fabric so you don't see the construction details.

FLATLINING This is the technique of sewing two or more fabrics together to create one fabric piece.

- *Interlining* is flatlined to the wrong side of the outside fabric and is added almost exclusively for warmth.

- *Underlining* is flatlined to the wrong side of the outside fabric to add stiffness and durability.

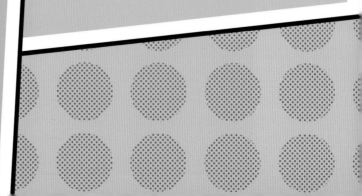

PATTERN AND SEWING TERMS

BASTING To temporarily stitch together two layers—fabric to fabric or trim to fabric. Basting stitches are usually removed. To baste, use a long stitch length on your machine.

BINDING Binding is the process of finishing the fabric edge of a garment with bias tape.

CLIPPING CURVES Curved seams require clipping into the seam allowance to minimize bulk and ensure the seams lie flat. Use the tips of your scissors to avoid clipping through the stitching. Clip into the seam allowance, perpendicular to the stitching, every ½″ or so depending on the shape of the curve.

DARTS Darts are used to help shape flat fabric into dimensional fabric pieces that hug the body. They are wedge-shaped folds of varying lengths stitched into a point. Darts are well marked on the pattern pieces, providing stitching guidelines.

EDGESTITCHING Visible stitching on the right side of the fabric, about ⅛″ away from an edge. Edgestitching is used for decorative touches or to keep the inside fabric from shifting to the outside of the garment.

FACING A small piece of fabric used to finish the curved edges of a garment. Facings are often used on curved seams like necklines, armholes, and collars. They are typically understitched to prevent the facing from rolling to the right side of the garment.

GATHERS Gathers are a series of soft folds in a garment. They are meant to sustain fullness and are often used in bodices, gowns, and skirts. To gather, run a long basting stitch across the fabric, leaving a long thread tail at both ends. Tie down one end and pull one thread from the stitch on the other side. You will see the fabric gather. Gather to your heart's content!

NOTCHES Notches are markings on the various pattern pieces that provide guides for matching two pieces together.

PLEAT A pleat is an overlapped fold in the fabric.

SEAM ALLOWANCE The seam allowance is the area between the edge of the fabric and the stitching line. Typically seam allowance is between ¼″ and ⅝″ for standard sewing, but if you think you will want to adjust the fit of a garment, you can make the seam allowance much wider.

STAYSTITCHING This type of stitch is done within the seam allowance to prevent the fabric from stretching while you are working.

TOPSTITCHING Topstitching, done ¼″ or more away from the edge, is meant to be visible on the right side of the fabric. It is used mostly for decorative purposes.

TRIMMING CORNERS Trim corners when you make a right-angle seam and you need to turn the item inside out. This removes the excess bulk of the seam allowances in the corners. Simply trim off the seam allowances at the corners on the diagonal, taking care not to cut the stitching.

UNDERSTITCHING Understitching is a form of edgestitching used to sew seam allowances to the facing or lining to help prevent them from rolling to the right side of the garment.

Pattern Prep

Now let's move to pattern and fabric prepping. A few steps before you start to cut and sew will save you a lot of time in the long run.

PREPPING THE PATTERN

Once you have determined your size (see Size, page 60), you might want to highlight the cutting lines on the pattern, especially if there are multiple sizes printed together. Depending on your project, you might want to be able to tailor the garment for a more custom fit. If so, consider cutting a larger size so you have extra fabric to take in or let out as you sew the pieces together.

Use craft scissors to cut out all the pattern pieces you need for your build. Be sure to follow the cutting line for the size you want to make. If the pattern has a lot of folds and wrinkles, you might want to press it carefully with a dry iron.

Pattern Mash-Ups

A common technique that many cosplayers use when crafting an outfit is *pattern mashing*. Pattern mashing involves taking two or more patterns and putting them together. I tend to do this when I am creating a gown or super suits; often one pattern will have the bodice I want but not the sleeves I want. So I look through my stash of patterns and pull the pattern with the sleeves that I want.

Pattern mash-up in progress in my studio

The trick to determining whether pattern pieces from different patterns work together is to "seam walk" the patterns against each other before you cut any fabric. To walk a seam, place the patterns on top of each other and align the seamlines. Pin the two pattern pieces together starting at the midpoint of a seam (bodice to sleeve; skirt to bodice, and so on). Hopefully the edges will match up and the two patterns will work together. If the seams do match up, move forward and use the patterns to cut your fabric. If they don't match up, see if you can gather up the pattern a bit or maybe add a pleat or a dart to make the pieces align. If this works, make sure to mark the pattern piece accordingly. This is your garment—you can do whatever you want!

> *"Make it work."*
> —Tim Gunn from *Project Runway*

Another consideration when you are mashing patterns is to make sure all the patterns you plan to use recommend the same types of fabrics. You can't mash up a pattern that requires stretch fabric with one that recommends woven fabrics that don't stretch.

Frequent pattern mashing will help you learn the look of patterns and mentally establish what a sleeve pattern looks like against a side front bodice piece. Mashing is a great way to gain more knowledge as you progress in your sewing journey.

TIP Don't forget to add seam allowances if you rework some of the patterns.

Muslin Mock-Ups

If you wish to make a muslin mock-up, now is the time—*before* you cut out your fabulous fabric. It's an optional part of the build, but if you need to try out certain shapes or you plan to use expensive fabric, making a muslin mock-up is a really good idea.

You don't have to make the complete garment. No need to finish necklines or add fancy trims. For the mock-up, simply stitch the basic pieces together, like the bodice front, bodice back, skirt front, and skirt back. From here, you can decide if you need to add more seam allowance to make the costume larger or if you want to add darts or gathers.

The more you alter the mock-up, the more you'll find you are deviating from the pattern. Adding darts, pleats, and gathers is totally okay to do, but doing so does change the way you

Muslin mock-up in progress

will need to sew the finished garment. This is diving into pattern making, which is whole other skill. If you are interested in pattern making, you'll need to do some research. Look at fashion pattern making books or view a fashion designer's YouTube channel, such as Nick Verreos's. Nick Verreos is a *Project Runway* veteran, and his videos are a great way to learn more about draping and pattern making.

If you do make changes to the muslin mock-up, you need to use the muslin pieces as the patterns. Use a seam ripper to open the seams, press the muslin mock-up garment pieces, and use those pieces as your patterns to cut out your main fabric.

Prepping and Cutting Fabric

Now your pattern is ready (lengthened, shortened, extra seam allowance, addition or removal of pleats and darts, any changes to the pattern clearly marked). Before you start cutting your fabric, there are some steps you should take to make sure your fabric plays nicely for you.

Since most fabric is dyed (and the dye might bleed in the laundry machine or on your skin) and some fabrics shrink, it is a good idea to prewash all but your dry-clean only fabrics.

Most fabrics can be machine washed, but check the fiber content to determine the water temperature and whether you can use high heat in the dryer. For more information, see Appendix A (page 123).

I recommend washing different types and fiber content fabrics separately. I also suggest either hanging your fabric to dry or using a low heat setting. Once the fabric is dry, press it to remove any wrinkles.

Now you can lay the pattern out and start cutting.

LAYING OUT THE PATTERN

Refer to the pattern instructions for the most efficient way to position your pattern pieces on your fabric. The instructions show cutting layouts for various fabric widths to help you best optimize your fabric yardage.

Typically, you lay out your fabric folded lengthwise with the right sides together so you can mark any design lines (like darts or pleats) on the wrong side. Make sure that the grainlines printed on the pattern pieces are parallel to the selvage edge. The *selvage* is the manufactured woven edge of the fabric. Don't use this edge in your pattern layout—just use it as a starting point to define the grainline and to line up your pattern pieces.

CUTTING AND MARKING THE FABRIC

FOR LONG, STRAIGHT EDGES, I suggest using a rotary cutter and self-healing mat to cut the fabric. Use fabric weights or pins to keep the fabric from shifting while you are cutting it.

TIP Pattern weights can be anything from sandbags to cats! I use cheap washers that you find at any hardware store. I highly recommend these for your sewing room.

FOR SMALLER-SHAPED PATTERN PIECES, pin the pieces to the fabric and use sharp scissors to cut them out.

Once all your pieces are cut out, use a fabric marking pen or tailor's chalk to transfer (copy) any design lines or other markings from the pattern piece onto the wrong side of the fabric. You might want to leave the pattern pieces pinned to the fabric until you need to use them, or else label them on the wrong side because patterns can have a lot of different pieces.

TIP If the right and wrong side of the fabric looks the same, use the chalk or fabric marking pen to mark the wrong side of each piece. Then you won't get confused when sewing!

Sewing the Pieces

*Once you are ready,
it's sewing time!*

Sew the pieces step by step according the pattern instructions. Some of the instructions can seem difficult to understand, so take your time and allow yourself to make mistakes. Search online tutorials on YouTube or on different sewing forum websites such as PatternReview.com. This is a great site with real opinions about commercial patterns, along with photos of garments created with the patterns.

Get into the habit of pressing seams as they are sewn, either open or to one side. This will allow the pieces to lie nicely against the body without bulk.

As you start to join larger pieces together, try them on or fit them to a dress form that's your size. Keep in mind that you should try on your garment multiple times as you make it to ensure the correct fit. Trust me on this!

TIP

When you finish your garment and are ready to mark the hemline, have a friend help. Stand tall, look forward, and have the friend mark where you want the hemline as you wear the garment. Friends make great sewing tools!

EMBELLISHING

Once your garment is sewn together, you are happy with the way it fits, and you love the look, it's time to add that special extra punch! Let's dive headfirst into embellishing your cosplay. Embellishing is one of my favorite things to do in cosplay creation. You can really get creative and express a lot of passion through tiny hand stitches or machine-stitched embroidery. There are so many ways to embellish, and there is an amazing variation of trims, appliqués, embroidery, beading, decorative stitching, and rhinestones. Experiment and discover your favorite embellishments to create your own personal style.

COSPLAYER:
Casey Renee Cosplay
COSTUME:
Sakizou Amethyst

Types of Embellishments

Embellishments can be virtually anything. If you can stitch it, glue it, fuse it, or hammer it on, it's an embellishment. This is a time to be truly creative with your cosplay. Have fun and try out anything that comes to mind. The embellishment shopping aisles can get vast and expensive, so keep your ultimate look in perspective. Grab that hot glue gun and hand-sewing box, and bling out your cosplay!

TRIM

Trim is a broad term for all types of materials used to embellish garments and accessories. They are usually sold by the yard and include ball-and-tassel fringe, bias tape, braid, cording, lace edging, piping, ribbon, rickrack, rhinestones or beads on a tape, and all kinds of variations of this list.

I personally like creating my own trims from items like fabric selvage edges and old Christmas wrapping ribbon. Trim tends to be costly, so save your coupons and experiment with buying swatches or a small amount of trim. Pin or hand sew it to your costume to see if you like the look before you buy yards of a trim that might not match your vision!

Many trims have an edge or lip so they can be machine stitched in place. Rickrack is simply stitched through the center. Other trims, like cording or pearls, can be couched in place (page 85). Bias tape and other narrow trims can be machine stitched over an unfinished garment edge. Many sewing machines have specialized presser feet that are designed to making stitching trims in place easier. Go to the internet or your owner's manual to see if you can purchase specialty presser feet for your sewing machine—you'll love them!

TIP

Making your own trims is often a big part of making your own costumes, but learning to make them takes time and practice (see YouTube and any number of books for how to start). For your first few builds, you might want to start with ready-made trim.

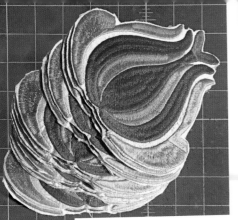

APPLIQUÉ

An *appliqué* is shape of fabric—think of it like a patch—that is typically created with fancy needlework, decorative topstitching, or machine embroidery and can be sewn directly onto your garment, accessory, or project. You can get very creative making your own appliques with hand or machine embroidery.

TIP

Combine appliqués with embroidery stitches for an extra-special look. For my Anastasia project, I created some blooming flower appliqués and fused them to the edges of the gown. I then hand stitched around the appliqués to add depth and detail to the hemline.

BEADING

Beading gives any garment a decorative edge. You can find beads in variations of stone, plastic, bone, shell, and pearl. Your beading can be the simple addition of single or clustered beads, or an elaborate beaded design.

Beading needles are long and thin—nice to have but not necessary if you have a fine needle that will go through the bead. Nylon beading thread is thin so you can use it on even the smallest of beads. Use a backstitch to attach beads.

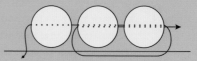

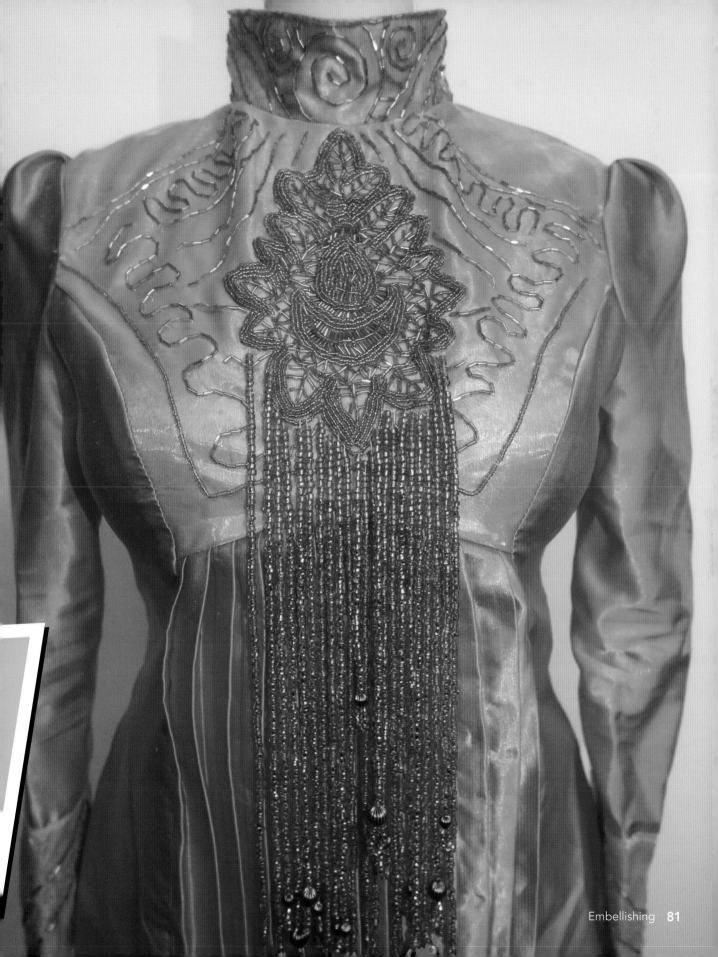

Distressed armor by Jedimanda as Wonder Woman

DISTRESSING

Distressing is an easy way to give a costume a weathered look. I use acrylic paints to distress fabric, armor, boots, or anything, really. Brushing on paints and wiping them with a paper towel, or even your finger, will leave behind a smudge. With practice and patience, painting on distressed details can give a garment a cool edge.

You can also use tea baths to lightly dye fabric to a darker brown color. Use dyes to dip different gradient looks onto fabric. You can even burn the fabric, but please use caution. Test burn a scrap of the fabric first before doing it on your fabric yardage or even your garment.

DECORATIVE STITCHING

One of the simplest ways to add a decorative aspect to your fabric is to use the stitches that come with your sewing machine. Most modern machines have multiple decorative stitches that are built into the machine. They are stitched in rows or straight and curved lines, and are often used by quilters. I used decorative machine stitches on my Doctor Strange cosplay and it's one of my favorite aspects of the build. I used random stitches as well as parallel rows of zigzag stitches in multiple thread colors.

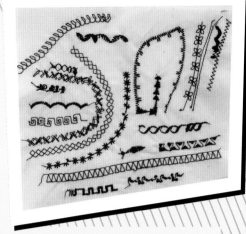

Try stitching all the different stitch selections your machine has on scrap fabric so you know exactly what you can stitch and which stitches you like best. Try stitching running stitches on top of each, or parallel to, each other. Try multiple stitch lengths with shorter stitch widths. Experiment with these decorative stitches, and you'll be amazed by their creative potential.

EMBROIDERY

Embroidery is the act of decoratively stitching with yarn or thread on larger pieces of fabric. It is an art form that has been perfected over thousands of years. Any type of thread or yarn can be used, from silk thread to cotton thread, and they produce very different looks. Hand embroidery is fun, easy, and inexpensive. There are specialty sewing machines and embroidery-only machines that are capable of computerized motif embroidery, but they are quite expensive. I highly suggest you fill a Pinterest or mood board with pictures or samples of embroidery and decorative embellishments for further inspiration.

HAND EMBROIDERY

Special needles, threads, and other tools will make it easier to create a wide range of stitches. These stitches (next page) will allow you to do some amazing hand embroidery. You can also use hand embroidery to attach pearls, sequins, beads, and jewels to your garment.

Hand Embroidery Tools

An **EMBROIDERY HOOP** keeps tension on your fabric so the fabric doesn't shift and the stitches don't pucker. Insert your fabric between the two hoops and keep the fabric taut. Hoops are made of metal, wood, or plastic and are available in several sizes. They are always in a circle or oval shape.

EMBROIDERY NEEDLES have large eyes (making them easy to thread with thicker threads and floss) and sharp tips. They come in a range of sizes from 1 to 12; the larger number, the smaller needle. A variety pack is a good place to start.

Choosing the **THREAD**, **YARN**, or **FLOSS** you want to use is a creative adventure! Embroidery floss is a common choice. Most floss is made of six strands; try dividing it into three strands to make it easier to use. Other embroidery threads include perle cotton, tapestry wool, cotton embroidery yarn, and even metallic and decorative threads, which are found on spools near the regular thread.

An assortment of **FABRIC MARKERS**, **SMALL SCISSORS OR SNIPS**, and **THREAD CONDITIONER OR WAX** finishes out your hand embroidery tool kit.

Hand Embroidery Stitches

BACKSTITCH   Using the same motions as a running stitch (page 35), this stitch resembles a solid line. Start by forming a straight stitch, but bring the thread to the right side a stitch length away. Reenter the fabric where the last stitch ended.

CHAIN STITCH   Start with a small straight stitch. Bring your thread and needle straight up through the fabric one stitch length away; slide the needle under the stitch and back down where the needle came up. Pull the thread through to form a loose loop (not taut). Bring the needle back up through the fabric and through the loop and continue. Your stitch should start to look like a chain. Repeat this motion.

COUCHING   Couching is a useful technique in which you lay one yarn or thread on the fabric surface and use a couching thread to secure it in place. Simply take small straight stitches over the top of the trim or heavy yarn that you are securing to the fabric. Try to space the couching stitches evenly.

FRENCH KNOTS   A French knot is a decorative stitch that leaves a little knot on top of the fabric. It's super cute! To do it, bring the needle and thread up through the fabric. While one hand is holding the needle in place, use your other hand to wrap the thread around the needle. Hold the wraps and insert the needle back through the fabric near its origin.

RUNNING STITCH   A running stitch is a series of evenly spaced straight stitches. It is a simple in-and-out stitch.

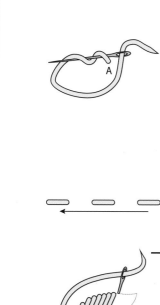

SATIN STITCH   Satin stitches are used to fill a motif or pattern. They are a group of closely placed and parallel straight stitches.

MACHINE EMBROIDERY

Machine embroidery is different than machine decorative stitching—it does require special sewing/embroidery or embroidery-only machines. I love it because it is much faster than hand embroidery and I can be doing something else while my machine is stitching the embroidery design.

These machines come preloaded with several alphabet and number fonts and appliqué designs. All you do is choose a design and set the machine to stitch it for you. If you want to design your own embroidery and machine stitch it, you'll need to purchase partnering digitizing software for your computer. The software allows you to convert a JPEG, bitmap, or PNG file into an embroidery file that your machine can read and stitch onto your fabric. I did this on three of my more famous cosplays: Queen Amidala, Doctor Strange, and Anastasia. I recommend visiting stores that sell various brands of these machines so you can try them before you buy—they are an investment.

COSPLAYER: Jedimanda
COSTUME: Doctor Strange from *Doctor Strange*
A. LEE STUDIOS

RHINESTONES

Rhinestones give the ultimate sparkle to your garment and can be sewn or glued in place. They come in all shapes, sizes, and colors. Most rhinestones have a flat backing so you can glue them in place; I recommend using a glue called Gem-Tac (by Beacon). It doesn't dry immediately so you have time to move the stones around before the glue dries (and it dries clear). You can purchase a tool kit with the proper tools for setting stones: a beeswax-tipped stick, a glue syringe with multiple tips, and glue. I recommend getting a small plate for the stones so you can pick them up with the beeswax-tipped stick and transfer them to the glue spot on your fabric.

You can also use Hotfix rhinestones. These rhinestones come pre-glued and require a special setting tool. Once you press the stone down with the heated tool, the glue activates and adheres the rhinestone to the fabric. This option works great if you are embellishing a three-dimensional project like shoes because you can place the stone within the tool and then press it in place.

There are several brands of rhinestones:

- High-end rhinestones are from Swarovski and Preciosa (my favorite). They have the largest and most radiant sparkle, come in different sizes categorized by the millimeter, and have different sparkle aspects. The AB, or aurora borealis, rhinestones appear to be different colors when lights hit them at different angles. They are pricey, but less so if you purchase them in bulk. Several websites sell these by the gross. A gross is 144 pieces; a great deal if you need a lot of stones.

- Craft stores have cheaper options that don't shine or sparkle as much as the Swarovski and Preciosa rhinestones, but they are certainly suitable for many costumes.

FINISHING TOUCHES

Congratulations! You've finished sewing and embellishing your cosplay, but there are a few more steps to help you best present your cosplay to the world.

A Final Look

Place all your garment pieces either on a dress form or on a hanger, step back, and examine everything. Does the cosplay need anything? An extra embellishment? Maybe another waistband or belt?

Once you are satisfied, I recommend getting super close with a pair of scissors or snips and snipping any thread tails left from the sewing machine. I always find some that I didn't catch. Also look for any tails of hot glue or seams that look loose. This is the time to fix anything. Finally, run a lint roller all over the garment to remove any threads, fuzzies, or animal hair.

Now it's ready for a final press and packing.

Ironing

Ironing is the essential final step. As a cosplay competition judge, I always mark down costumes that haven't been properly ironed because, in my opinion, that garment isn't finished yet. For competition work, your cosplays need to be finished, and you really don't want a wrinkly garment to hinder your final presentation to the world.

A good iron has multiple heat settings, which is important when you are working on different fiber fabrics. It is also important that the iron has a steam function to help further press out tough wrinkles.

COSPLAYERS: Sewcialist Revolution and Evil B Costumes
COSTUMES: Queen Elizabeth II and Prince Philip, Duke of Edinburgh from *The Crown*

IRONING, PRESSING, AND STEAMING

Ironing is the act of gliding a hot iron across fabric to release wrinkles. Don't be afraid to use steam when you are ironing to help release those wrinkles easier.

Pressing is the act of placing a hot iron down on fabric—not moving it—to press in a fold or a crease. You can also hit the fabric with a shot of steam to help release stubborn wrinkles.

Steaming is done using a *steamer* and is perfect for removing wrinkles without having to put the garment down on an ironing board.

IRONING SUPPLIES

It's nice to have a dedicated location to store your ironing supplies. You need an iron, ironing board, water for steam pressing, and pressing cloths. A pressing cloth is a medium-sized scrap piece of muslin or cotton fabric for you to sandwich between your fabric and iron. You never know if your fabric will melt a bit or the heat will leave a funny texture, so test by pressing first with the pressing cloth. You can remove the pressing cloth if there aren't any marks and the heat setting is okay.

You might also find a tailor's ham, sleeve board, and iron cleaner useful.

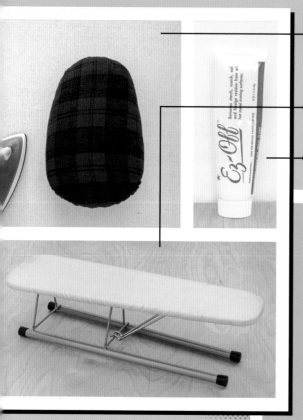

- A **TAILOR'S HAM** is a dense pillow filled with sawdust that is used under the garment to press a curved seam. The ham is meant to mimic different body curves.

- A **SLEEVE BOARD** is narrow board that makes it easy to press sleeves.

- **IRON CLEANER** helps remove residue from the metal plate.

WILL IT BURN?

Yes, fabric does burn. But it burns or scorches differently depending on its fiber content. As we discussed before, cotton and polyester fibers make up a large portion of the fabric options available for home sewists. Polyester fabric will melt and shrink up. Cotton fabrics won't catch fire but can leave a burn mark on fabric if the iron is too hot. To prevent this from happening, use a pressing cloth and make sure your iron is set to a setting that is suitable for your fabric. There really isn't anything to be afraid of with ironing, so you really should iron your garments. Just don't touch the metal plate or you will burn some skin.

Packing and Storing

One of the questions I am asked most frequently is how I travel with my cosplays. The short answer is that I try not to, mainly because I'm terrified of losing my luggage and because my costumes are large and require a lot of suitcases. But it's okay! You can't let fear hold you back, so find the largest suitcase you can. Preferably, you'll want a hard-case piece, but those can be expensive. Some of my cosplay friends travel with heavy-duty lockable cases and storage bins. Keep in mind that you often fly to cosplay events, so search the website or contact the airline's customer service center for checked-bag guidelines.

I love to use garment bags for storing and traveling with my cosplays. Most of my cosplays are sewn pieces and can hang on hangers. I tend to keep my accessories in bags that I place inside the garment bags. Keeping your garments in bags also protects them from dust and scents that can attach to fabric. Attach a list to the garment bag of the all the items you need for the cosplay so you don't forget anything. For a bonus, throw a dryer sheet or two into the garment bag to keep your costumes smelling fresh and clean.

COSPLAYER: Jedimanda
COSTUME: Doctor Strange from *Doctor Strange*

COSTUME TRAVEL

Cosplayers travel with weirdly shaped items that security may want inspect. Just in case your luggage is opened, place a typed letter stating that you are a costume artist traveling to *[insert your destination here]*. Add a photo of the costume and information about what it's made of (foam, metal, fabric, and so on). Finally, add your contact information. This helps security understand what's in your luggage so it is less likely to get held back for further investigation. (No fun!)

See Appendix B (page 125) for a sample letter.

WIGS
AND
SHOES

Wigs have been worn throughout history, for protection from the elements, for status, or to sport the latest high-fashion trend. And shoes—well, everyone loves a great pair of shoes!

COSPLAYER: Silhouette Cosplay
COSTUME: Daenerys Targaryen from *Game of Thrones*

Wigs

Wigs are becoming one of the most popular cosplay accessories, and in some cases a necessary one, to help pull off your character's look. Wigs aren't always necessary, and I know a lot of people that don't care for them, but I find them a super fun cosplay accessory.

COSPLAYER: Jedimanda
COSTUME: Lydia Deetz from *Beetlejuice*
WIG: Synthetic wig created by Amanda Haas using wig pieces, foam, and wire

COSPLAYER: Jedimanda
COSTUME: Cersei Lannister from *Game of Thrones*
WIG: Created by Custom Wig Company using human and synthetic hair

WIG FIBERS

Regardless of their function, wigs are made from three different sources or materials: animal, human, and synthetic.

Animal-Hair Wigs

Animal-hair wigs are typically made with horse, sheep, or yak hair. These fibers can give a wig extra volume and are usually expensive. Unless specified by the wigmaker, you won't see a lot of animal hair in wigs used for cosplay. If you are looking for historically accurate wigs, then most likely you'll want to find a wig made using animal hair and historical wig-making techniques.

Synthetic Fiber Wigs

Synthetic fiber wigs are the most common type of wigs worn among cosplayers. They are the least expensive to purchase and are available in the most styles. The hairs are made of plastic fibers, so you can't use a styling tool that heats up unless the wig label indicates it is heat resistant. If you place a hot curling iron near most synthetic fibers with the intention of curling the hair, the hair melts and burns. Heat-resistant wigs can be styled with tools that heat up. Just make sure your wig specifically says if it is heat resistant if you intend to style it

with a hot curling iron. If you can't use a hot curling iron on your synthetic wig, look up different methods to style wigs that aren't heat resistant, such as the boiling water or steam methods. Synthetic wigs come in a hard front or lace front (see Types of Wigs, page 96).

Human-Hair Wigs

Human-hair wigs are also common, but they are not as common as synthetic wigs because they are more expensive. Human-hair wigs are made from human hair sourced from hair untainted with dyes or products. The hair is typically hand tied onto lace to create the wig. These wigs are super customizable and often seem like wearer's real hair. It's the perfect option if you truly want to dive into a character fully. The human hair wig is a considerable, but worthwhile, investment.

For more information on human hair and custom wigs, refer to Resources (page 126).

COSPLAYER: Jedimanda
COSTUME: Ariel from *The Little Mermaid*
WIG: Synthetic hard-front wig
from Gothic Lolita Wigs

TYPES OF WIGS

Hard Front

A **HARD-FRONT WIG** is created with an edge towards the front of the wig that is typically covered with bangs or short hair. They are the least expensive type of wig and contain mostly *weft*, rows of hair sewn together and then hand stitched into the wig. With weft comes a lot of volume; these wigs tend to be heavy. They can be made from human, animal, or synthetic fibers.

Lace Front

A **LACE-FRONT WIG** is a combination wig with hard-front workmanship in the back of the wig and soft lace (hand tied or dyed hair) workmanship from the crown of the head forward to the forehead. This option gives the wearer more of a natural look for the hair-line. A lace-front wig is more expensive than a hard-front wig, but it is a popular option for cosplayers. These wigs are easily styled and come in many colors, lengths, and styles. These are some of my favorite wigs; they lay nicely under crowns or head wear, and can be made of human, animal, synthetic, or a combination of human and synthetic hairs and fibers.

COSPLAYER: Jedimanda
COSTUME: Jean Grey from *X-Men*
WIG: Synthetic-lace front
from Wig is Fashion

Full Lace

A **FULL-LACE WIG** is created completely
with human hair and/or synthetic fibers that
are hand tied onto lace; sometimes it's even
custom fit to the wearer's head shape and
hairline, making it is easy to style and even
restyle. Often used for short-hair men's
wigs and heavily styled wigs, a full-lace wig
is ideal when you need a realistic style. It
is the most expensive type of wig, but if
you repeat a character often, this might be
a great option for you. Full-lace wigs are
typically difficult to purchase online; you'll
probably need to contact a professional
wig designer and maker if you want a full-
lace wig.

COSPLAYER: Jedimanda
COSTUME: Princess Anastasia
from *Anastasia*
WIG: Full human-hair lace wig
created by Custom Wig Company

STYLING TOOLS

Some wigs, like long curly ones, can be pulled out of the bag, shaken, and worn. Most wigs, however, need some styling, in which case you'll need some styling tools.

The more you style wigs, the more supplies and tools you will gather.

- Gels and hairsprays (göt2b hairspray and style gel [by Schwarzkopf] are my favorites.)

- Combs, including a wide-tooth comb, fine-tooth comb, looped wig brush, rat-tail comb, and teasing brush

- Sharp shears

- Pins, including wide-hair pins, bobby pins, T-pins, and yellow-headed pins

- Hair clips and ties, including alligator clips, double-prong clips, rubber bands, elastic hair ties

To display and style your wigs, you'll want the following:

- Wig stand
- Canvas or Styrofoam head
- Rollers, curling iron, hair dryer, and straightener
- Steamer for styling heat-resistant synthetic wigs

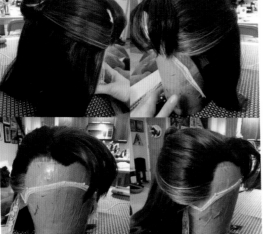

TIP From anime to fantasy, popular cosplay characters can have some crazy hairstyles. If you are confused about how to style a character's hair, you should search the web for tutorials. A lot of cosplayers willingly share their tips and tricks on wig styling and typically record their process. Don't be afraid to experiment or reach out for help. A wig can always be restyled unless you cut it.

Shoes

All complete outfits need shoes, right? Yes, they certainly do! You do need shoes for your cosplay if you are attending a convention. I will say I don't do much to my shoes except repaint them on occasion. Of course, this all depends on the outfit. Some cosplays require *greaves*, which is armor for your shins. For my Captain Marvel cosplay, I created "boot socks" and added the armor that stretched over my foot and hung on my legs. For my Wonder Woman cosplay, I glued armor to old boots—it worked great!

COSPLAYER: Jedimanda
COSTUME: Captain Marvel
from *Captain Marvel*

COSPLAYER: Jedimanda
COSTUME: Wonder Woman
from *Wonder Woman*

PAINT RECOMMENDATIONS

Repainting shoes is super easy if you use leather paints. Leather paints have an elasticity that prevents the paint from chipping. Moving, flexing, and stretching causes normal acrylic paints to crack and chip off. See Resources (page 126).

TIP

I recommend Angelus leather paints; they are the absolute bomb for repainting shoes. And they come in tons of colors and shades! Plaid and DecoArt also have leather paints at a cheaper price point, but I suggest adding more layers of those paints if you use them because they tend to thin out.

SHOE SHOPPING

Some great places for cosplay shoe shopping are thrift stores because you are probably going to be chopping up, painting, or decorating them. Be careful about buying shoes that aren't well made; you don't want to sacrifice comfort for price. I hate going to cons and finding almost immediately that my feet hurt. If your character wears giant spiked heels and you are worried about walking in them or just worried about them being uncomfortable, try to get wedges in the correct color. Wedges put less pressure on the ball and heel of your foot, so they are easier to walk in for long periods of time.

See Resources (page 126) for some shoe-shopping suggestions.

TIP

Sometimes insoles can help if you find your feet hurt. Try Dr. Scholl's inserts. It might be a good idea to keep a pair in your bag.

CONVENTION TIME

Most of the time, cosplayers congregate at conventions. *Conventions*, or *cons* for short, are gatherings that happen worldwide with a common theme based around a fandom or genre of fandom. For example, San Diego Comic-Con is based mostly around comic books, and PAX East is based around video games. But other conventions like Star Wars Celebration or D23 Expo are based around Star Wars and Disney fandoms, respectively.

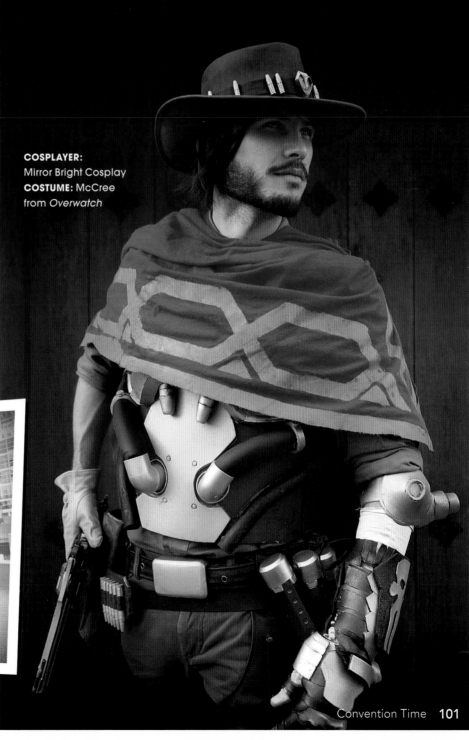

COSPLAYER: Mirror Bright Cosplay
COSTUME: McCree from *Overwatch*

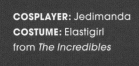

COSPLAYER: Jedimanda
COSTUME: Elastigirl
from *The Incredibles*

FANDOM TYPES

Typical fandoms include:

Comic books

Anime

Video games

Tabletop gaming

Science fiction

Fantasy literature

Horror films

Multi-genre cons that combine two or more fandoms

COSPLAYER: Jedimanda
COSTUME: Yang Xiao Long from *RWBY*

COSPLAYERS: Jedimanda, Sarah Dempster, LunarLyn
COSTUMES: Queen Amidala and her handmaidens
from *Star Wars: Episode I—The Phantom Menace*

Where and When

Conventions happen all year round and are typically held in larger cites with convention centers capable of holding a lot of people. But there are also smaller conventions that are held in hotels, museums, and even high school gyms. My first convention was Derby City Comic Con 2012, a tiny comic book–centered convention that launched my interest in cosplay.

You don't have to produce a super cool cosplay to attend a convention, but I guarantee that if you attend a con in your cosplay, you will have the best time. People from all ages, backgrounds, and fandoms attend these, and cosplay is one of the highlights. Attendees love taking photographs with their favorite characters, and that could be you!

What to Expect

Con days can be long, so prepare—especially if you are cosplaying. Wear comfy shoes if you can, or take a lot of breaks to rest. Plan to eat! I know that may sound crazy, but it's easy to the go the whole day without eating (a bad habit!) when in costume because the day can be enjoyably hectic. Pack some small snack bars or plan to leave at a certain time for food. It is not fun to be at a con with a headache because you are hungry and dehydrated, so drink lots of water! Staying hydrated is key to lasting a long time in your costume. I realize it is kind of hard to hide water bottles in your costume, but having a handler or buddy hold a bag with water in it is ideal. If you are going alone or if everyone is in costume, bring a small drawstring bag or a bum pack with a water bottle. If you can't eat, at least stay hydrated. You can create your own Bum Bag to store your essentials while cosplaying (page 120).

If you are in a costume, no matter who you are portraying, someone will want your photo. It's the absolute truth. You could be seven feet tall, on stilts, and have wings, or be rocking a purchased costume from Party City—someone will still want a photo. That said, *it's up to you if you want to be photographed.* This is the first thing I tell new cosplayers at their first con in costume. If you want to pose for photographs, strike your best pose and go for it! If you prefer not posing for photos, that's fine too. Most people will respect your wishes.

In costume, you will also probably run into some very excited fans. There might be superfans of the character you're portraying, and for them, seeing their character in real life is exciting and sometimes overwhelming. Superfans can be children or adults. They can also be shy or extremely talkative. Most fans will ask for a photo, thank you for the photo, and move on, but some might want to talk to you. Children especially might want to talk, or they might just stand and look at you. It's strange at first, but it's part of the cosplay world. I tell new cosplayers, especially if they are a character that is popular with children (like Disney princesses), to take care to maintain the magic for them. Most of us aren't actors, so it's hard to be that character or stay in that character while speaking.

Me chatting with young Star Wars fans

Kids will just be excited to take a photo and say hello or goodbye, so do your best "princess speak" and wish them well. You will have made their day and possibly your own. Some fans might have a disability and interacting with them can be tough but rewarding. If any fan gets overexcited, just stay calm, talk to them, and allow a quick photo. Fan interaction is my biggest highlight of any con.

COSPLAY IS NOT CONSENT

Staying on the topic of photographing with fans, consent is an important word in the cosplay world. "Cosplay is not consent" is a movement that empowers cosplayers and fans to speak out about inappropriate behavior and interactions that happen at conventions, especially with cosplayers. Sometimes, a fan might think that just because you are dressed as his or her favorite character that they have the right to touch or say inappropriate things to you. This fan might have a strong connection to their favorite characters, and sometimes that line blurs a bit in real life and in their heads. They may come up for a photograph and place hands on you inappropriately or verbally harass you for some strange reason. I hate that this happens, but it does. I have had a handful of interactions like this, so it's important for me to spread the word that this isn't okay. Just because we are dressed as a character doesn't mean we are down for anything. Most conventions worldwide have this statement clearly displayed at their cons with a zero-tolerance policy. If you feel harassed or see someone being harassed, call security at the convention and inform them of the matter. Travel with a buddy or be with a group; be smart and stay vigilant. It's an unfortunate dark side of cosplaying, so we band together and prepare for anything. Cosplay is not consent.

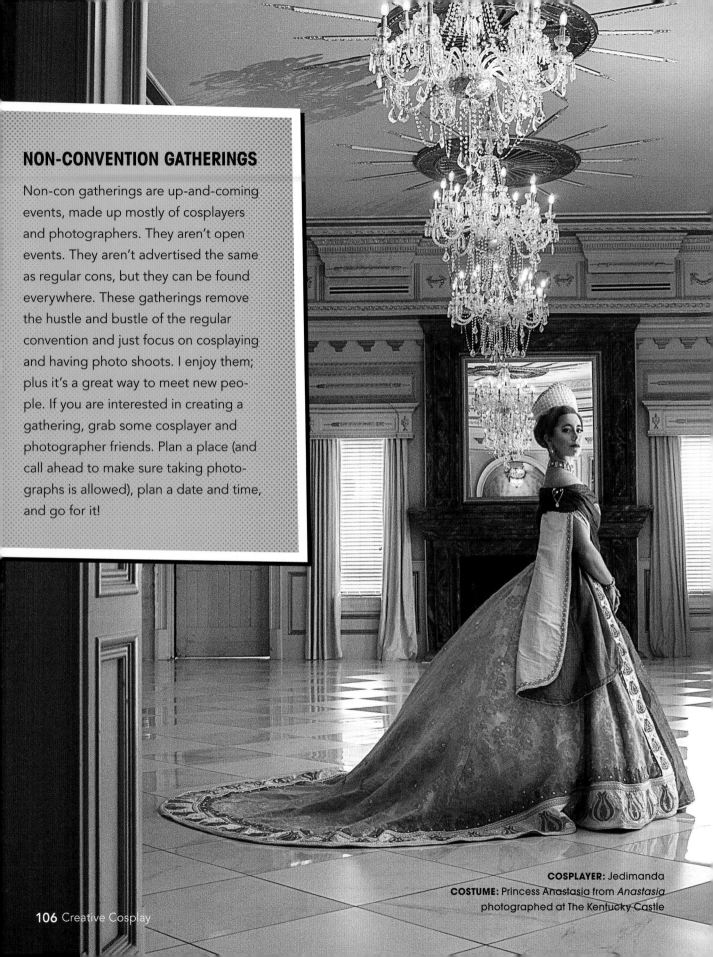

NON-CONVENTION GATHERINGS

Non-con gatherings are up-and-coming events, made up mostly of cosplayers and photographers. They aren't open events. They aren't advertised the same as regular cons, but they can be found everywhere. These gatherings remove the hustle and bustle of the regular convention and just focus on cosplaying and having photo shoots. I enjoy them; plus it's a great way to meet new people. If you are interested in creating a gathering, grab some cosplayer and photographer friends. Plan a place (and call ahead to make sure taking photographs is allowed), plan a date and time, and go for it!

COSPLAYER: Jedimanda
COSTUME: Princess Anastasia from *Anastasia* photographed at The Kentucky Castle

COSPLAY COMPETITIONS

Cosplay competitions are a great way to show off your work. Competitions are a completely optional aspect of the cosplay world, but competing can be extremely rewarding. Cosplay competitions, costume contests, and masquerades have been happening for years!

Best in Show at Gen Con 2017

COSPLAYER: Cowbutt Crunchies
COSTUME: Helga from *Tree of Savior*, Best in Show and World winner at The Crown Championships of Cosplay at C2E2 2019

What Is a Cosplay Competition?

Simply put, a *cosplay competition* is a contest that is often judged by professionals, putting cosplayer against cosplayer in certain curated categories to win a prize. At most conventions, it's the main event. I've competed and judged in front of hundreds, even thousands, of people. Convention attendees love watching the cosplay contests. The prizes can range from trophies, large and small sums of money, and recognition. It's the ultimate test of skill, acting, and/or craftsmanship.

Me competing at D23 Expo 2015

REGISTERING AND TYPES OF COMPETITIONS

The first step toward competing in a cosplay event is registering. There are several types of competitions, so it is helpful to understand the various categories before you register. You might want to look online to get a sense of what goes on at one. Here is a general description of the various cosplay competitions.

Skill/Craft-Based or Skit-Based Competitions

There are two main types of cosplay competitions: skill or craft based and skit based. Sometimes, depending on the convention, there could be a mix between the two, but for the most part they are separate. The skill/craft-based competitions are called *Craftsmanship Competitions*, and the skit-based ones are called *Masquerades*. Cosplays at both are usually judged on accuracy, craftsmanship, presentation, and audience reaction, although not all competitions judge audience reaction. It is up to the discretion of the convention planners and the judges whether they want to add any more criteria to the competition, and the criteria is usually indicated when you sign up to compete.

- *Accuracy* means how close the representation is to the inspiration character or design.

- *Craftsmanship* considers how well the cosplay was created.

- *Presentation* refers to how well the cosplay was presented to the judges; points awarded on finality (if your costume is completed or not) are judged here.

- *Audience reaction* is your stage presence and how the audience reacts to your cosplay.

These skill/craft- and skit-based competitions can be divided up into a variety of different categories. I tell folks to be honest and try to place themselves in the appropriate category. If you are an experienced craftsman but have never competed before, enter the journeyman or master categories. The judges have the power to bump you to another level if they see that you belong there.

Skill- *and* age-based competitions *are further divided up into kids, novice, journeymen, and master categories.*

- The *kids' category* is usually for children age twelve and under, but they can be different depending on the con. These younger contestants usually aren't judged against the rest of the contestants but have their own prizes and recognition.

- The *novice category* is intended for first-time costume makers and first-time cosplay competitors. This is often a large category and it is for first timers!

- The *journeyman category* is for repeat cosplay competitors that have yet to win a best in show. This category is one level up from novice.

- *Masters* are for professional and seasoned cosplayer and cosplay competitors that have won competitions or have placed high in final rankings.

Genre/Fandom-Based Competitions

Some competitions are divided by genre, or fandom. I see this mainly at certain fandom-based conventions like Star Wars Celebration, Gen Con, and D23 Expo. Genre categories can include anime, TV/film, fantasy/literature, video games, comic books, original designs, and potluck. *Potluck* is a mixed bag of cosplay contestants that doesn't fit into the other categories.

Costume-Based Competitions

Costume-based competitions usually feature the highest quality and toughest master-level competitors. The categories can include sewing/needlework, FX or special effects makeup, armor, and larger than life. These contests usually have an application process, and you must be selected to compete. Don't be discouraged if you don't qualify right away; it is good to have goals! I started competing in smaller cons and I worked myself up to competing in international competitions. By setting goals and working towards them, cosplay competitions become great achievements.

PREJUDGING

Once you are registered, there will probably be some time before the actual competition. Use that time to finish and perfect your cosplay.

The competition begins with a set time (usually between five and twenty minutes) for you to meet with the judges wearing your complete and final cosplay. This is an opportunity for the judges to chat with you and examine your cosplay before the stage portion of the event. This can be an intimidating time, but it's the best time to really tell the judges how you made your outfit. Since you won't be sure how long you will be with the judges, prepare what you want to say and how you want to say it.

No matter the type of competition, *bring references or a portfolio of inspirational images and work-in-progress images to show the judges.* The judges need to know what inspired you so they can judge the accuracy of your costume. I tell people to be creative; your portfolio doesn't have to be a book or presented professionally, but it should include references of your character and of you creating the garment. Good judges can see if you made your cosplay or if you didn't, so make sure to reference all the pieces you have created in your portfolio. It also helps to have your images arranged in the order that you want to present them to the judges. This helps you stay on track and minimizes saying *um* and *uh* too much. Your *prejudging time*, or time with the judges, is crucial and is your opportunity to really show off. It's your cosplay—be confident and proud!

YOUR PREJUDGING TIME

- Arrive ten or fifteen minutes ahead of your time slot.

- Use the bathroom before your time slot for bathroom needs and last-minute touch-ups.

- Freshen up with gum or mints.

- Talk slow, but be aware of your time allotment.

- Save some time for the judges to ask you questions, and let the judges know you have allowed time for questions. The more you all talk together, the more they will remember you.

THE STAGE SHOW

The stage show is different for craftsmanship contests and masquerades.

FOR A CRAFTSMANSHIP-BASED COMPETITION, the stage show typically is called a *walk on*, which means you get between 30 seconds and 1 minute to work the stage. You enter from one side of the stage, strut around the entire stage, and exit the other side of the stage. Usually the announcer reads text you prepared ahead of time about your cosplay, and there will probably be music playing while you gallivant across the stage. This is the best time to work your audience. Strike some poses that the character usually does, and work your garment if you have a cape or gown train. Twirl to your heart's content, but control your twirling. Use your props to their fullest extent, and smile! Do not yell or try to speak over the announcer unless you have permission to as part of your stage presence. Don't rush your stage time. It's so easy to get caught up on stage, so listen to the announcer and he or she will tell you when to exit.

Photos by The Portrait Dude

Amanda Haas winning the Central Champion regional award at the Crown Championships of Cosplay at C2E2 2018
Photo by The Portrait Dude

FOR A MASQUERADE COMPETITION, you must perform a skit. Personally, I've never entered a masquerade and performed a skit, so I don't have as much information about this type of cosplay, but I do know it is absolutely necessary to nail your skit! Depending on the masquerade, you can sing or lip sync, dance solo or with a group, or even perform scenes from your inspiration for the audience. Prior to the contest, you must have your skit planned and provide music to the contest staff. This takes a lot of practice! Masquerades are truly amazing to watch. The contestants put their hearts and souls into their performances on that stage, and it's an honor to watch.

Once the stage show is finished, you have to wait for the judges' decisions. This takes a while because the judges deliberate and carefully consider all the cosplayers. Typically, there are reserved seats in the audience for the contestants, but they can also wait back stage. This part is nerve racking, but it's the part we contestants all wait for. Once the judges have completed their deliberation, the announcer or judges call the category competitors back to the stage and announce the winners. It's an exciting time!

POST-COMPETITION PSYCHOLOGY

It stinks to lose. No one likes to lose! However, what matters most with these competitions is that you enjoy them. Being on stage, twirling, and posing are the truest forms of showing off. Be a good competitor and don't be a sore loser. If you don't place in a category, that's okay! There will always be another contest to enter. Congratulate the winners and move on. Don't hound the judges about why you didn't win; accept their decisions and move forward. It's the experience that you gain from entering these events that makes you a better competitor, not how many trophies you've carried off the stage. Keep competing and keep getting inspired by your fellow competitors. Talk shop backstage and learn from each other. Being backstage is honestly my favorite time as a cosplay competitor.

COSPLAY PHOTOGRAPHY

Cosplay photography is an emerging and fast-growing art form. People have been photographing cosplayers for years, but in the past decade professional photographers have lent their talents to the cosplay community. Many have found success and are able to make a living shooting cosplay. There are different types of cosplay photographers, and it is important to be aware that not all photographers have your best interest in mind.

COSPLAYER: HDC Fabrication
COSTUME: Varian from Zach Fischer's Project Ebon Blade

Expectations

Anyone can take a photo, and many people at these conventions do. There are fans/attendees that take pictures with anything from their iPhones to DSLR cameras. They sometimes will tag you in their photos on social media for you to share.

There are "hall-shot photographers" that are there specifically to take one or two photos of you and move on. Most will tag you on social media or email you the photo at no cost if you provide them with your information. Some hall-shot photographers are there to beef up their own portfolio, so you might never see the photos they took of you. This happens a lot.

Photo Shoots

Then there are professional photographers and videographers that also attend the con. They are there to book and organize photo shoots, and they make a living photographing your newest cosplay creation. If you want to set up a photo shoot during a convention (or anytime), you can find professional cosplay photographers via social media, their websites, or through cosplay colleagues.

I know photo shoots aren't for everyone. They can be uncomfortable, and honestly, most of us have no idea how to pose or what to do with our hands. But as cosplayers, we play the game of creating and wearing amazing costumes. Even if you do not post anything online, I guarantee you are still going to want a photograph of your cosplay.

Outside photo shoot with Alexandra Lee Studios

Building a cosplay portfolio is an ideal way to track your work and your creative growth. You put a lot of hard work into your cosplays—why not show them off in photographs? A good photographer, if they know what they are doing, will help you display your cosplay at its fullest potential. Having professional photos of your work also allows you to share them online while giving credit to the photographer, of course. With great photos comes great share-ability!

When you find a photographer, ask about his or her rates to make sure you can afford the photo shoot before committing. Photographers, like cosplayers, are artists, and their work deserves payment. Some photographers ask for the funds up front; others have payment plans. Photographers also offer solo and group shots at different rates, and it is up to you and the photographer to decide on the number of final photos included in the photo shoot fee. You will probably need to sign a contract (see the interview with Alex, page 118, for more information on photo rights).

Finally, different photographers do different levels of editing after the photo shoot. Some perform a basic natural-looking edit, while others will go to a higher level of editing: a composite or photoshop level. Make sure you find the right photographer that can photograph you the way you want. You want to love your photographs! Look at their portfolio and any online photos from competitions and other events before signing a contract.

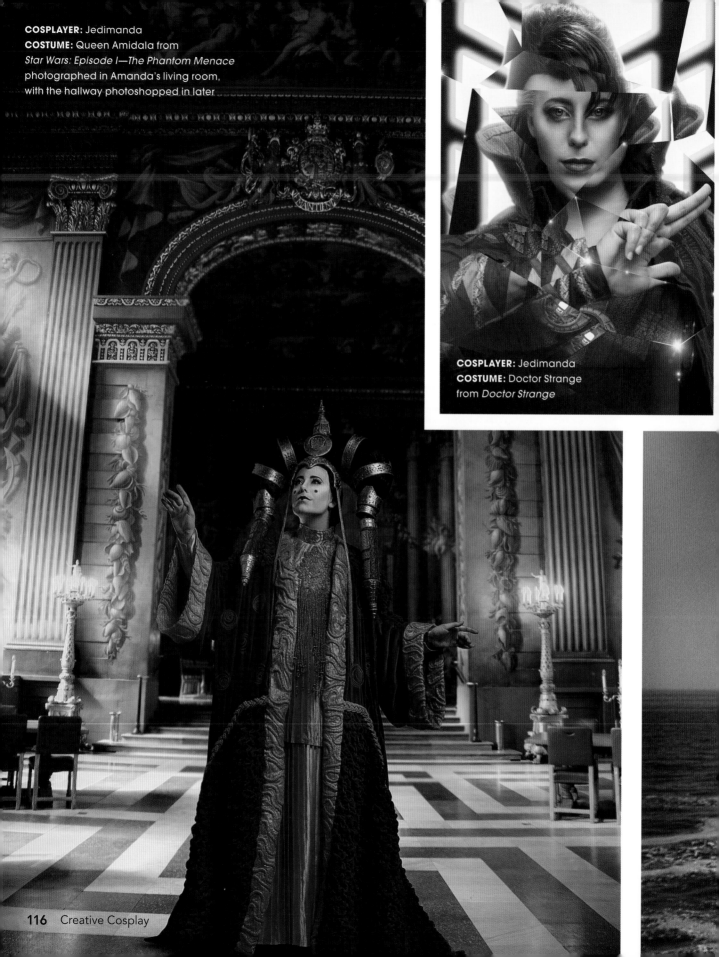

COSPLAYER: Jedimanda
COSTUME: Queen Amidala from
Star Wars: Episode I—The Phantom Menace
photographed in Amanda's living room,
with the hallway photoshopped in later

COSPLAYER: Jedimanda
COSTUME: Doctor Strange
from *Doctor Strange*

COSPLAYER: Malicious Cosplay
COSTUME: Seaking variation from *Pokémon*

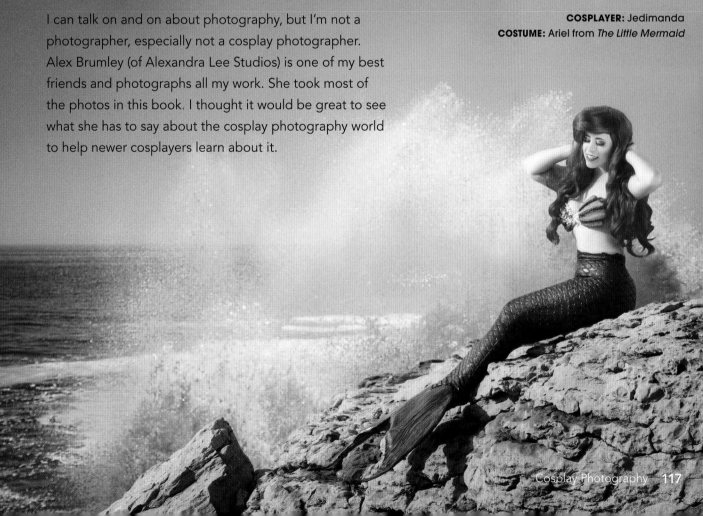

I can talk on and on about photography, but I'm not a photographer, especially not a cosplay photographer. Alex Brumley (of Alexandra Lee Studios) is one of my best friends and photographs all my work. She took most of the photos in this book. I thought it would be great to see what she has to say about the cosplay photography world to help newer cosplayers learn about it.

COSPLAYER: Jedimanda
COSTUME: Ariel from *The Little Mermaid*

INTERVIEW WITH COSPLAY PHOTOGRAPHER ALEXANDRA LEE STUDIOS

Can you give a brief background on your path to cosplay photography?

Hi! My name is Alexandra Brumley. I go by Alexandra Lee Studios in the cosplay and photography communities, and I'm a full-time cosplay portrait photographer. I discovered cosplay photography while I was still focusing on commercial and fashion portraits. However, I have always been a huge fan of pop culture, so I was immediately drawn to cosplay photography. I've been taking cosplay portraits for six years and I have no intention of stopping.

As a fan of fandoms, were you drawn to cosplay photography because of a certain fandom or the artistry around costuming?

I was working as a fashion photographer because of the artistic freedom it provided. So, when I discovered that cosplay photography was a thing, I jumped into it immediately. The way I see it, cosplay is just another version of fashion—a nerdy fashion.

When working with a cosplayer, how do you help them pose and stay in character?

Before a photo shoot, I research the character and create a mood board. By the time the photo shoot comes around I'm fully prepared. One of the things I tell my models during the shoot is "nose goes," which means they should be looking wherever their nose is pointing. This makes for a more dramatic-looking photo and also minimizes how much the whites of their eyes show, so they don't look frightened or uncomfortable. I also tell them not to hold a pose for too long. There is a sweet five- to ten-second zone once the pose is made that looks natural. After that, the model starts getting stiff or starts thinking about the current pose, which can show in the camera.

Do you prefer studio or location shoots?

I love both of these but for different reasons. Studio shoots are fantastic for larger or difficult-to-wear costumes because the model will be in a more controlled environment. If I am photographing a heavy and hot cosplay, I blast the air conditioning and have the fans ready. If a model can't walk easily in a costume, the studio is perfect because I can position the model in front of the backdrop and set up lights strategically. Location shoots are equally as fun because I can take a great variety of shots with more movement.

Do you have a favorite location?

Oh man, that is a hard one! One of my favorite locations was the Mountain Cosplay Retreat up in Birken, British Columbia. The mountains and glacier-fed lakes are absolutely breathtaking, and I would go there again in a heartbeat.

Once the shoot is over and you move on to the editing process, how much enhancement or editing do you do to the photographs?

I've designed different editing packages for my photo shoots. There are shoots where all I do is retouch the skin and add a color gradient over the images. However, I also specialize in composite photography, where we might shoot at a convention or studio but the resulting photograph shows the model floating with sixteen arms in space, about to take down a titan. Basically, it depends on what my client is looking for.

Can you speak about photography rights in terms of what you can do with your photo after you're finished editing?

Photo rights, or photo copyrights, differ for each photographer. Ultimately, when I press the shutter button on the camera, I am the sole owner of that photo—no

Alex Brumley of Alexandra Lee Studios

matter if it was a paid shoot or a photo-for-time (PFT) shoot. The only time a photographer is not the copyright owner of an image is if it was contractually stated prior to the shoot. For me personally, I don't have a lot of rules on what you can or cannot do with my images. You can post them to social media if you give me and the model credit. Business cards and banners are also fine. It's only when a client wants to sell my images that we need to sit down and talk. I allow clients to sell my images as long as they pay for a printing license. A print license is essentially a written document that states that you have permission from the copyright holder to sell the image. Terms and conditions for print licenses varies between photographers, so definitely read the fine print!

Do you believe that photography can help a newer cosplayer improve their skills and grow as a cosplayer?

Oh, I definitely think there are aspects of photography that benefit cosplayers. Photography, I believe, uses a different kind of creative eye and makes you see things differently and artistically. At the same time, it can also help cosplayers see themselves from different angles and helps them hide things that they don't want seen in photos.

How do you see cosplay photography growing in the future?

The cosplay photography community is growing everyday with more accessibility to cameras. What's really going to be exciting to see is how the art of cosplay photography grows as photographers go above and beyond with their subjects. Personally, I love compositing and special effects editing for cosplay photography. I would like to start adding 3-D modeling effects into my work.

MAKING A BUM BAG FOR CONS

FINISHED BAG: 10˝ wide × 5˝ high × 2˝ deep

MATERIALS

- ½ yard of fabric for bag
- ½ yard of fabric for lining
- ½ yard of fusible interfacing (if needed)
- 7˝ zipper
- 1 yard of piping (*optional*)
- Decorative trim (*optional*)

You Will Need

- Paper for pattern
- Ruler
- Chalk or fabric marker
- Scissors or rotary cutter
- Sewing machine
- Zipper presser foot
- Matching thread
- Iron with steam option
- Pressing cloth

Making the Pattern

Pattern piece measurements include ½˝ seam allowances.

1. Make the following pattern pieces:

11˝ × 6˝ rectangle for the front and back panels

3˝ × 31˝ rectangle for the sides (or 3˝ × 15½˝ for half of the pattern)

3˝ × 3˝ square for the belt tabs

2. Mark the zipper location the panel pattern piece. Measure 1½˝ from one long edge and mark a centered line the length of the zipper teeth.

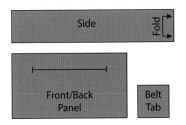

CUTTING THE FABRICS

- From the bag fabric, cut 2 panels, 1 side piece, and 4 belt tabs. (If you made half of the pattern for the side piece, place one end on a fabric fold for cutting.)

- From the lining fabric, cut 2 panels and 1 side piece.

- From the interfacing (if using), cut 2 panels, 1 side piece, and 2 belt tabs.

TIP If you choose light- to medium-weight fabric for the bag, you might need to add a layer of interfacing. I recommend using medium-weight fusible interfacing. The interfacing adds strength and structure to your bag over time.

Making the Bag

Use a ½˝ seam allowance unless otherwise noted.

1. Fuse the interfacing (if using) to the wrong side of the panels, side pieces, and 2 of the belt tab pieces, following the manufacturer's instructions.

TIP I finished all the edges of my pieces with a serger, mainly because my fabric was already fraying and that bothers me. If you choose to serge the edges, now is the time to do it.

2. Place and pin the panels and side piece to their corresponding lining pieces, wrong sides together. Sew ¼˝ from the edges.

3. Place and pin 2 belt tab pieces (1 with interfacing, if using) wrong sides together, and sew ¼˝ from the edges. Stitch an X across the center. Fold and press under the edges ½˝. Topstitch 2 opposite sides ¼˝ from the edge. Repeat to make 2 belt tabs.

4. Cut on the marked zipper-placement line on the panel pattern piece. Place the pattern on a fabric panel piece and mark the zipper placement.

5. Stitch ¼˝ from the marked line to attach the bag fabric to the lining at the zipper opening. This makes it easier to turn in the edges to stitch in the zipper.

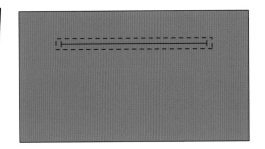

6. Cut on the marked line, stopping about ½˝ from each end. Snip diagonally into the corners.

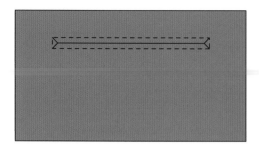

7. Press the edges of the zipper opening to the lining side. Use a pressing cloth to protect the fabric.

8. Center the zipper under the opening. Using a zipper presser foot, edgestitch about ⅛˝ away from the zipper teeth to sew the folded edges to the zipper. Make sure that the zipper will be able to open and close easily. Press.

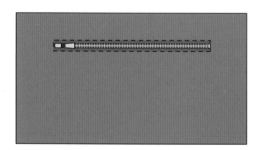

9. Join the ends of the side piece together. Press the seam open.

10. With the seam at a corner, pin and sew the side piece to the front panel. Clip the side piece and lift the presser foot to pivot the fabric at the corners.

11. Position the prepared belt tabs on the back panel, measuring 1˝ from the top edge and 1½˝ from the sides. Stitch ¼˝ from the top and bottom edges to attach the tabs.

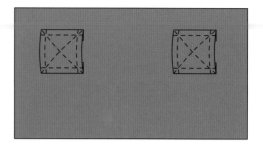

12. Open the zipper about halfway. Pin and sew the other edge of the side piece to the back panel, clipping and pivoting at the corners as before.

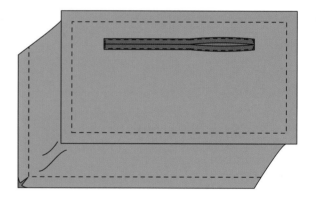

13. Trim the excess seam allowance diagonally at the corners. Turn the bag right side out through the zipper opening.

Now you can slide the bum bag onto any belt for any cosplay. Happy cosplaying!

APPENDICES

APPENDIX A: FABRIC CHART

FABRIC	COSPLAY POSSIBILITIES	PREWASH	TIPS
Brocade	Ball gowns, corsets, jackets, capes, trim	**Silk:** Dry clean only. **Polyester/cotton:** To soften	Brocade's heavy weight is great for embroidery.
Chiffon	Petticoats, dresses, skirts, blouses	**Silk:** Dry clean only. **Polyester/cotton:** Hand or spot wash.	Chiffon layered with lace gives costumes an airy look.
Dupioni	Corsets, bodices, skirts, ball and evening gowns	**Silk:** Dry clean only.	The bumpy/knobby texture works as a contrast against shiny/smooth fabrics.
Felt	Accessories, backings/stabilizers	No	A good choice to use underneath fabrics to puff them up for 3-D texture.
Jersey	Dresses, skirts, shirts, pants (4-way stretch)	Yes, to preshrink, soften, and remove excess dye	Available in a variety of patterns, colors, and textures, and both 2- and 4-way stretch
Lace	Overlays on dresses, ball and evening gowns, trims, appliqués, collars, cuffs	No	Try dyeing and layering lace over many different fabrics for a multidimensional and vintage look.
Leather	Jackets, capes, tops/bodices, pants, accessories, belts, shoes, gloves	No	Use a specific leather needle while sewing leather.
Linen	Shirts, pants, skirts, dresses, capes, jackets, corsets, undergarments, linings	Yes	Use linens for your basic undergarments because they absorb moisture quickly and will help keep you cool.
Muslin	Shirts, pants, skirts, dresses, capes, jackets, corsets, linings	Yes, to preshrink	Use muslin for draping and testing patterns; then use the same pieces to construct the lining.

FABRIC	COSPLAY POSSIBILITIES	PREWASH	TIPS
Organza	Petticoats, dresses, skirts, blouses, accessories	No	Use organza to line skirts and add body without using a heavy petticoat.
Quilting cotton	Shirts, pants, skirts, dresses, capes, jackets, corsets, linings	Yes, to preshrink	Quilting cottons come in different colors and patterns. Use them for fun linings.
Satin	Ball and evening gowns, shirts, pants, skirts, dresses, capes, jackets, shorts, corsets, linings	No	Satin is a classic fabric for gowns, but try using it as a base for embroidery. Stabilize the fabric first.
Shantung	Corsets, ball and evening gowns	**Silk:** Dry clean only. **Polyester/cotton:** Hand or spot wash.	Use shantung as a contrast fabric with dupioni. Both have similar strength and durability.
Spandex	Superhero suits, pants, leggings, tightly-fitted shirts, gloves	No, unless needed to remove excess dye	Use a ballpoint/stretch needle.
Suede/ Ultrasuede	Jackets, capes, tops/ bodices, pants, accessories, belts, shoes, gloves	No	Suede and Ultrasuede are incredibly durable and will not lose color over time.
Suiting	Suits, shirts, pants, shorts, jackets, capes	**Polyester/cotton:** Yes	Suiting fabrics fray like crazy; finish your edges quickly after you cut.
Taffeta	Ball and evening gowns, petticoats, skirts, corsets, dresses, accessories, trims	No	Pins easily mar taffeta. Use a fresh needle every time you stitch on taffeta.
Tulle/ netting	Petticoats, accessories, trims	No, unless needed to clean	Tulle and netting do not fray; make sure your cuts are final and even.
Twill/duck	Corsets, linings, undergarments, accessories	Yes, to preshrink and soften	Twill and duck canvas can fray easily; treat the edges as soon as you cut.
Velvet	Bodices, corsets, capes, jackets, coats, pants, shirts, collars, cuffs, accessories	No	Use a special presser foot (Teflon, roller, or walking) so you don't leave tracks on the fabric.
Vinyl	Jackets, capes, tops/ bodices, pants, accessories, belts, shoes, gloves	No	Place tissue paper under the presser foot and sew over it for easier stitching.
Wool	Coats, jackets, capes, accessories, trims	No	Wool scorches easily; use a pressing cloth.

APPENDIX B: COSTUME TRAVEL INSERT

Hey there! I bet you're curious about the weird shapes within my checked luggage. I am a professional costume artist/cosplayer that travels often with my costumes. Below is information on the costume that you may need to conduct your search.

Date: _____ / _____ / _____

Cosplayer name: _____

Convention I'm heading to: _____ in

_____ , _____

Phone number to call if you have questions: _____

Home address if luggage is lost or misplaced: _____

Here are some photos of what you are seeing:

Please be careful moving the costume pieces around because some are very fragile and need to be handled with care.

Please pack the luggage back up in a similar way that I previously have packed it.

Thank you!

_____

COSPLAYER: Jedimanda
COSTUME: Queen Amidala from *Star Wars: Episode I—The Phantom Menace*

RESOURCES

Fan Art

deviantart.com • tumblr.com

Full-Costume Outfits and Pieces for Original Cosplay

amazon.com • ebay.com • etsy.com • ezcosplay.com
miccostumes.com • procosplay.com • whitesheepleather.com

Fabric

dharmatrading.com • fabric.com • fabricdepot.com • fabscrap.org
fabricwholesaledirect.com • joann.com • moodfabric.com • spoonflower.com
silkbaron.com • spandexhouse.com • spandexworld.com

General Craft

amazon.com • dickblick.com • hobbylobby.com
jerrysartarama.com • michaels.com • walmart.com

Custom Wigs

Custom Wig Company   customwigcompany.com

This is a shameless plug, but this is where I work every day. We create high-end custom wigs for clients. From Santa Claus to Cersei Lannister, an 1870s women's updo to a classic Elvis wig, we can do it all. Check us out!

Cosplay Wigs

ardawigs.com • customwigcompany.com • dolluxe.com
epiccosplay.com • posewigs.com • wigisfashion.com

Shoe Shopping

amazon.com • thredup.com

Leather Paints

angelusdirect.com • decoart.com • plaidonline.com